To Arnie & Anita

parhain terveisin

Arizonasta

THE FINN IN ME

3/4/06

Smileka G. Garcia

# THE FINN IN ME

## IN ME

*The Chronicles of a Karelian Emigrant*

by

Sinikka Grönberg Garcia

North Star Press of St. Cloud, Inc.

**Library of Congress Cataloging-in-Publication Data**

Garcia, Sinikka Grönberg, 1931-
    The Finn in me : the chronicles of a Karelian emigrant / by Sinikka Grönberg Garcia.
    128 p. 23 cm.
    ISBN 0-87839-070-7 : $9.95
    1. Garcia, Sinikka Grönberg, 1931-    . 2. Finnish-Americans—Biography.  3. Karel 'skia A.S.S.R. (R.S.F.S.R.)—Biography.
    I. Title.
E184.F5G37   1992
973'.049454102—dc20                  92-15442
[B]                                    CIP

Published by North Star Press of St. Cloud, Inc.,
P.O. Box 451, St. Cloud, Minnesota 56302.

Printed in the United States of America by Versa Press, Inc., East Peoria, Illinois.

ISBN: 0-87839-070-7

*I dedicate this book to my family in the United States:*
*Chico,*
*Dina, Lisa,*
*Quique, Tom,*
*Kayla, Raakel, Monique,*
*Kyle and Marko*

## Acknowledgements

In Finland, my thanks go to my sister Anja, whose enthusiasm about the Finnish version of my story got me going, and to my classmates, who found my book more interesting than the books they got for Christmas.

In this country, my thanks go to Kathryn (Kater) Nelson (Anonsen), who gave me the idea of contacting North Star Press, and to Rita, Corinne, and Rose Dwyer, who found a way for my book, and, above all, to Richard Holmes, my friend, editor, and cartographer.

Sinikka Garcia
Tucson, Arizona, 1992

# Foreword

During the first year of my early retirement from teaching at Catalina Foothills Schools' elementary schools, after twenty-five years work, I sat down and wrote my story. Based on a good memory and extensive diary-keeping from 1944 to 1988, the first version was in Finnish. It was sent, chapter by chapter, to my mother in Finland. From her, the circulation expanded and received much response and caused me to write it in English for my family here in Tucson.

The *New Yorkin Uutiset*, a Finnish-American newspaper, in their special commemorative issue on *The Winter War*, published the parts of my story dealing with World War II and the loss of Karelia, my childhood province, to the Soviet Union.

# Contents

THE FINN IN ME

Finland, showing the places of my childhood and adolescence.

*Chapter 1*

# Under the Northern Lights

**Before August 1939**

Värtsilä was a village in the eastern part of Finland known as Karelia, which since World War II has belonged to the Soviet Union. The name appeared in some Russian documents as early as in the 1500s. Counting the surrounding farming community, 6,000 people lived in Värtsilä in the 1930s, which was a thriving community due to the Värtsilä Concern's Iron Works (established in 1884) that provided work and benefits to its workers. Värtsilä had active social and cultural groups—a community theater, several choirs, bands, a string orchestra, and sports teams—and was situated in the best agricultural region in Finland. Winters were cold, summers warm.

I, Sinikka Grönberg, was born on one of those forty-below-zero nights in January 1931 when the northern lights flashed their eerie veils in the sky. The night had been busy for Mrs. Halmetoja, the county midwife; before bringing me into the world, she had delivered a baby boy, Martti, to his family in the next apartment building. Besides our birthdays, Martti and I had good singing voices in common; we became partners singing duets in our primary school.

I'm told I was an infant of perpetual motion, fussing and sleeping but little and driving my parents crazy. Early in life I also developed an allergic eczema that made my life and that of those around me that much worse with my itching and scratching.

I soon knew that everything in Värtsilä connected with the Iron Works. Everybody's father worked there. Everybody's home, the sauna, the wash-house, the cows, the horses, the school—everything belonged to the Works. The Iron Work's siren ruled our lives. When it went off at 4:00 PM, my brother Juhani and I hurried home to hide for our Dad to find us—usually behind the wooden sofa in the kitchen.

I also learned that there were four kinds of people in Värtsilä: factory

1

workers, farmers, storekeepers, and bosses, all with Swedish names as Åhman, Wahlfors, Kuhlefelt and Mattlar.

Now, fifty years after leaving Värtsilä, all the summers of my childhood seemed warm and wonderful for playing and swimming, and all of my winters were of deep snow, freezing, and excellent for skiing, sledding, or for snow-castle building.

My world in Värtsilä stretched from the rectory that stood close to us, to the elementary school on the hill in the center of the village. However, I was most familiar with the immediate area where I lived. I knew that behind the rectory was the yellow railway station and behind it the huge, white iron bridge which connected us to the big cities of Viipuri and Sortavala.

On the main road stood three magnificent family housing developments called Pihkalinnas, "Pithcastles," the newest and best of the Iron Works-owned projects. Two stories, and made of flat-surface logs painted red, they housed eight families each. We lived in the first one between the Skutnabbs and the Olkkonens. Our apartment was on the second floor. The roofs of the Pihkalinnas were of red, curvy tile, and all the windows and door frames had been painted white. We had a roomy living room where some of us slept. It had a blue-gray wooden floor, a kitchen with a

My home "The Pithcastle."

large brick oven and a stove, an alcove and two foyers. The upstairs foyer had the pantry, and from there the stairs led to the attic. Attached to the living room was a balcony. A long, straight staircase connected the upstairs and downstairs foyers.

Each family had a woodshed and outhouse—a long row of them stood in the backyard. Between our building and the next house was a huge, round tub of water used only in case of fire. Water was brought to it in barrels on the top of a horse-drawn cart. The same type of transportation took care of emptying of the outhouses.

Every family had a garden plot for growing peas, beets, carrots, rhubarb, and potatoes. Many summer mornings when I awoke, I was scared, for Mother wasn't at home. She had gone down to weed her garden. On pleasant summer evenings people got together on the neighbor's bench to chat. My mother loved that more than anything. Between the Pihkalinnas was plenty of room for children's play, and an enormous wall without windows for playing individual ball games.

In my family were my father, Eino; my mother, Maj-Lis; my brother, Juhani; my sister, Anja; my grandmother, Miina-Mummo; Uncle Arvi; and I.

Uncle Arvi had the alcove to himself where he kept the most interesting things—a drawing board and blueprints, a set of triangles and compasses, a slide rule and rolls of paper. Juhani, Anja and I were not allowed to touch any of it. A graduate of a technical school and a foreman at the Works, Uncle Arvi owned a blue comb that folded in half like a jackknife. Juhani and I loved taking turns in combing his light brown hair with it while he lay comfortably on the wooden sofa in the kitchen. Our pay came in the form of butterscotch candy.

Miina-Mummo or simply Mummo was the mother of my father, Uncle Arvi, and Aunt Linda. A soft and kind widow, Mummo dressed in long-sleeved long dresses—several layers of them in the winter. Her shoes came half way up her legs with long laces. She read the bible, feared God, and attended church on Sundays dressed in black. She taught me several songs, one about Black Sarah, which says that there was no danger in dying, no tears, and no night in heaven. She attended all school events with me.

Mummo suffered from rheumatism. She slept on the top of the wooden sofa—the board removed and placed between two chairs—and her feet in the lower oven! Mummo and her husband, Heikki, had been poor farmers; Mummo was very frugal in everything. Dad used to tell us about his cap that had been patched several times over. After they sold their farm, Heikki and Mummo moved to Värtsilä, where Grandpa took a job at the Iron Works.

One day in the winter of 1936 I accompanied Mummo on a chair sled (kick sled) to the hospital to see Uncle Arvi, who was ill. On the even parts of the road I sat, and Mummo did the driving. On the uphills I walked, and, on the way back from the hospital, I squatted on the runners behind the seat and in front of Mummo's feet to feel and enjoy the speed of the "Doctor's Slope" better. But, when Mummo kept using her foot as a brake to slow down and since she wouldn't listen to my protest, I got up from my squatting position and took command of the vehicle. At the same time I

"Doctor's Slope."

also knocked off Mummo, leaving her on the road while I continued the ride. Frightened by my own action, when the chair sled came to a stop on the bridge, I fled! Instead of going back to see Mummo, I took a side road home.

That evening Dad did his duty by spanking me with a birch switch on my bare bottom. I myself brought him the switch from its usual place on the door frame and, after half a dozen strokes, obediently apologized for what I had done. The most humiliating part was to say, "Forgive me, *dear* father, I'll never do it again!" Spankings were not frequent at our house, but I do remember a few of them, and at times I felt totally wronged. Mummo's eye, injured in the fall, underwent several color changes—from black to green to yellow—before it got well again. After the incident, every time visitors came, the story was told, and no matter how hard the people tried keeping a serious face, I knew they were really amused.

Juhani, my brother and two years my junior, was a "good" boy; he played nicely by himself, ate well and looked well-fed. I, on the contrary, was always on the go, a finicky eater, and skinny. One winter when Juhani's tongue got stuck on a frosty door handle, I ran to Mother with the news. She knew just what to do and in no time had released his tongue by pouring water on it. How enticing to the tongue frosty metal is! I had experienced the same thing with a frosty ax in the backyard, but no one was around to hear my agony, and I had to carry the frozen ax stuck to my tongue until I was rescued, suffering a very sore and bloody tongue.

My mother, Maj-Lis Malin, was nineteen when I was born. Tall and slender, she had shining dark hair and classical features, a stunning contrast to the typical, shorter, blonde local women. Mother spoke both Finnish and Swedish since she was from a Swedish-speaking region in southern Finland. One day Mummo hired her to teach her son (my dad) some Swedish; a romance sprang from it, and Dad never learned his second language.

Mother was the oldest of the Malin girls: Maj-Lis, Anni, Greta, Viola, and Hjördis (Jöppe). Since there were no boys in the family, Maj-Lis was her papa's helper when they went fishing at Åminnefors by the Gulf of Finland. The Värtsilä Iron Works had invited Pappa Malin to come to Värtsilä; that's why the Malins came.

In Mother's memory Pappa was a tall, gentle man who drank unrefined spirits when nothing better was to be had. He died young of a burst stomach ulcer in Värtsilä, leaving his family in great distress. After his burial, Mother took a job at the Iron Works' gardens.

Mother soon gained the reputation of having a bad temper—based on the impression company housing director Åhman got when paying a visit to the Malins. Of medium height, Åhman behaved like a general. He had come to evict the Malins since Pappa no longer worked at the Works. After listening to Director Åhman's message, Mother replied that although she wasn't the head of this family, her family was not about to move anywhere. "Director Åhman, there's the door!" and she pointed it out to him.

Later when Director Åhman heard about Dad's intentions to marry Maj-Lis Malin, he warned him about the young lady's temper.

Mummo helped Mother bake *sultsinas* and Karelian *piirakkas*, individual rice-pies. Sultsinas look like rice rolled in tortillas. Piirakkas are little oval boats with rice showing in the middle. The shells for both were made of rye and wheat flour. After cooking the sultsinas on the stove and the piirakkas in the oven, they were basted with melted butter—and were delicious. Mother added cardamom to the "pulla" dough—braided coffee bread loaves—and cinnamon rolls that were called "ears" because of their shape.

On Friday nights Mother took us to the company sauna where she beat us gently with a softened, fragrant bundle of birch branches to help cleanse us inside out. After warming up on the top bench of the hot room, we'd be sure to have one hand in the fresh water bucket when more steam was produced in the heater—to splash water on our faces and hair.

Because my father was thirty-two at the time of my birth, our family somehow had an easier start. He was different from most workmen. Although a welder, he dressed and behaved like a gentleman. Dad dressed carefully in the best quality clothes for which he paid cash. Always neat and clean, he worked hard, did a lot of overtime, and saved off the top of his earnings. He did not smoke or drink. Brandy was kept for medicinal purposes only. Every Friday, payday, Juhani and I would bring out our banks and deposited a *markka* into each.

Dad had worked as a magazine salesman on the side and had earned many sets of silver spoons in fancy, satin-upholstered cases and books for his bookcase. Among the books were Goethe's Works, a set of encyclope-

dias, Sillanpää novels, and a series of picture books on the provinces in
Finland, which we read along with him. In one of the books was a picture
of a country lad with his pants half way down as he was hurrying to the
outhouse. We got such a kick out of that picture that we always wanted to
see it first.

When Dad bought a 1932 model Ford in 1936, he also equipped himself with a chauffeur's cap, a special dark blue suit, a pair of fine riding boots
and long-sleeved gloves. The car was dark blue on the outside and gray on
the inside, and it smelled of excitement just as the Gramophone did. Once
in a while Dad gave someone a ride somewhere, but I mostly remember
seeing him under the car fixing endless flats. Toward the end of his car
ownership, Dad injured a cow, and the incident became a court case. If anything positive came of the war, it was that Dad never went to court but sold
the car just in the nick of time.

It was quite remarkable for a welder to own a car in 1936 in Värtsilä.
The bosses of the Works had their cars and so did two or three taxi drivers.
No one else.

Adding to Dad's status as gentleman-worker, our summer cottage was
completed in the summer of 1939 at Lake Jänisjärvi, where the well-to-do
had their villas. Ours was a simple one-room cottage with a sauna attached.
I remember the wonderful smell of new wood, of perking coffee, pulla, and
playing on the shore with water lilies bobbing on the waves.

My mother's mother, Anna Malin, lived at Alatupa, a long, old building, with her single daughters, Greta, Viola and Hjördis (Jöppe). The building had a dark, long foyer from which the doors of six apartments opened.
Mamma's home had a tapestry on the wall depicting exotic animals in the
forest. She had dainty porcelain figures and statuettes, copper kettles and
coffee pots on the shelves. Mamma's brother had been a sailor and had
brought her many things from foreign countries.

Mamma was tall and slender like my mother, and her thick, wavy hair
was prematurely gray and tied in a bun. Since she was from Åminnefors,
her language was Swedish, and her Finnish was poor. She had a large wine-
colored birthmark on her right cheek. Everybody called her "Mamma
Malin," although her name was Anna. After her husband's sudden death,
Mamma started to work at the Iron Works, making wire.

From Mamma's house one could see the white Lutheran Church at
the crossroads and two older housing projects. Every time I crossed the
road to visit Maila Kralin at the Rämsäs, I walked through a clearing that
had been a market place. Many crooked-rooted pines formed neat "rooms"
in which we played with pine cone horses and cows. We were intrigued by
stories about Gypsies who used to camp under the pines; scared too because they were said to steal children. At times our parents resorted to
threats to give us away to the Gypsies!

*Chapter 2*

# In the Satchel Came the Babies

**July 11, 1936**

My sister Anja was born in July 1936 when I was five and a half years old. I knew we would be getting a baby because I had seen Mrs. Halmetoja, the midwife, go in with her leather satchel. We all knew that in that satchel came the babies. Also, Jöppe, my aunt, who was ten at the time, had been sent by Mamma to get Juhani and me out of the way early in the morning. We stood on the long bench in front of our house, waiting to be invited in to see the new baby. When the moment came, we ran upstairs to meet plump and beautiful Anja.

When Anja was one week old, our family took a trip in our Ford to Savonlinna, a town with a medieval castle, and to Massilanmäki some two hundred kilometers west of Värtsilä. First we stopped at Koli, one of the most scenic places in the whole country. Juhani and I liked best the endless stairs made of stone; we ran up and down them repeatedly. Another novelty for us was breakfast-in-bed. On the way to our destination we stopped to pick bogberries. I especially liked the acrid smell of the bog itself.

I used to think Anja was lucky to be born later than me, for bananas had reached Värtsilä by then. Our mouths watering in advance, Juhani and I would sit and wait for left-overs after Anja had been fed her banana. But one day Anja had a strong allergic reaction to them; she couldn't stop vomiting. Fortunately, a phone call made by the village pharmacist to Helsinki's Children's Hospital saved her; a few drops of glucose did it—and no more bananas for Anja.

**Summer of 1936**

Our neighbor ladies often bribed me with candy to sing for them. One summer day I was summoned from play to sing for some guests of theirs—

7

in the yard. I chose a tango that went, "One evening after our ship anchored
at the harbor of Rio Janeiro, all of us guys ran to the tavern of the old pirate,
where the most ardent women are and— heavens, what tangos are played
there! . . ." That time I was paid five marks in cash!

I probably had learned the song from Lempi, a teenager living in Uncle
Arvi's vacated alcove while attending the Värtsilä High. She was a blue-
eyed blonde, pleasant and happy—and someone for me to admire. From
her I learned that Nivea Cream on your eyebrows made them look darker
and kept them in line. Lempi also taught me to read and write before I
entered first grade. I learned my pop music repertoire from her. She could
be persuaded to play a few games of Black Peter with us, a card game similar
to and as exciting as Old Maid. I knew that Lempi had a boyfriend, for I
heard Dad scolding her one night as she came home late.

## January 1937

One winter the Iron Works constructed two toboggan runs that were
iced over during the night. One was for the bigger kids, the other one for
the smaller ones, and both were lighted for evening use. Although the runs
were meant for "belly sleds," we preferred sliding down on a piece of cardboard or without anything, sitting up or lying down. From the Iron Works
scrap metal yard we picked up large enameled shields that said "Shell" or
"Gulf," which worked well if they were round and saucer-like. Unfortunately the fun ended after the very first winter because the mothers com-
plained of the wear and tear on their children's clothing. But it was wonderful while it lasted!

## Summers 1936-1939

A typical summer activity was an excursion to the local sawmill to pick
up a load of scrap wood for our stoves and ovens. There were many of us,
even some grown-ups, each pushing his or her pushcart for a kilometer or
two. Children had carts specially made by our fathers. The wonderful
smell of moist earth and birchwood has stayed with me as a pleasant memory. It was a lot of fun to gather pieces of birch with as much bark on them
as possible; the more, the better, for birch bark started a fire easily.

## In 1936-1937

Aunt Linda, my father's only sister was a well-dressed modern person
in her thirties. She was my godmother. Though trained to be a barber, she
so abhorred her acquired trade from the very first bearded and unkempt
customer that she quit her job then and there. Instead she took up cooking
for private families in Viipuri, Sortavala and later in Helsinki. Once, when

she was working for a Värtsilä doctor, Mummo, Juhani, and I visited her, walking through the park-like garden to the impressive front door. Aunt Linda herself in her starched apron and hat welcomed us. She looked important. The doctor's home was stylish and spotless with expensive furniture, paintings, and crystal chandeliers.

Every time Aunt Linda and Dad met, one of them would say "Hurtishuu," and the other one would answer "Chickamentsaalaa!" Supposedly it was Gypsy language. They hugged and burst into laughter, which caused a general hilarity of which we never tired.

Aunt Linda had an admirer, Otto, who played the violin and to whom she had been engaged on the 15th of April, 1923, when she was twenty-three years old. That date was engraved on the 18-karat gold ring I inherited from her. Their break-up had had something to do with the violin and a serenade that had annoyed her. She had sent him away, not knowing that he would never return. Aunt Linda never quite got over her loss, and she never married.

Miina-Mummo, Sinikka, Aunt Linda.

## In 1937-1939

Across from our house was an old building called "Koulutupa" with tall fir trees on two sides. Behind it was the wooden hill that we used for downhill skiing. The fir trees by the main road were ancient and grew gray beards that hung down to the ground. Now and then we played house under them.

Koulutupa housed a common mangle for ironing or pressing sheets, pillow cases, and anything without buttons. It used neither steam nor heat. Sheets were rolled around very smooth logs—two or three at a time—and placed in the mangle. Then at the pull of a lever the heavy machine lowered onto the logs. Electricity made the logs roll back and forth, pressing the clothes smooth. Since I was the oldest child, I had the honor of helping Mother on the mangle trips. I loved to touch the smooth logs and to feel the cool, pressed sheets on my bed. I knew that the mangling of clothes was the final step in the laundry process and that it would be a while till the next washday.

In the evenings and on Sundays, the Salvation Army used the mangle room when conducting Sunday School classes and evening programs. We loved the Salvation Army people's cheerfulness and the interesting bible stories they told. The little kids got to handle cardboard camels and Bedouins in the sandbox that represented Palestine's deserts. The people sang and played their instruments—guitars, concertinas, and drums—with enthusiasm and taught us many songs. Sometimes they held raffles, which assured a full house. One time I won six pretty buttons for my doll's dress.

The Salvation Army people had military titles—major, captain, cadet. The ladies dressed in dark blue, two-piece suits with high collars and red and silver insignias. Their hats were hard bonnets with big black bows under the chin.

Our favorite times were the summer daycamps that the Iron Works paid for and which the Salvation Army conducted. We met by the lilac bushes in front of the headquarters at 7:00 AM to wait for the horse-drawn wagon that took us to the camp at Lake Jänisjärvi, or, since not all of us could fit on the wagon, some of us walked to the two kilometer marker. There some of the riders got off, and the walkers rode for the rest of the way. The horse, trotting most of the time, followed a familiar route: up the hill to the fork of the road by the church, past the cemeteries. Soon we reached the moor that cut the road in two. For the rest of the way, thick pine and fir forests grew on both sides of the road, obscuring the view until we arrived at the campsite and the beaches.

## Chapter 3

# Syllables and "Sal Ammoniac"

**September 1937 and 1938**

Värtsilä Concern, the Iron Works, also owned the nearby primary school and the fire station. From my house I took the main road to the Iron Works Road, then cut through the fire station yard to my school. Two grade levels occupied the same classroom: the first graders on the left, the second graders on the right.

For crafts we worked with clay and wove things out of *niini*, which, according to my dictionary, means "bast." It was straw-like but strong and burned my fingers when I pulled on it too hard. In several colors, it had an interesting taste and smell. We were also taught to sew buttons onto a piece of cloth—even the boys learned.

A tall, yellow and black abacus stood at the front of the classroom. Each pupil worked the beads in turn. Because the Finnish language is phonetic, reading was learned by sounding out the syllables. By the end of the book the print was small; you had learned to read "straight."

I loved to sing and to take part in plays. Martti, the boy who was born

Värtsilän tehdas, the factory.

the same night as I, and I were often chosen to sing duets; we even performed in musicals.

At the edge of the school yard lived a shoemaker who sat on his leather-topped barrel nailing heels and sewing soles. From time to time some of us girls would stop by to ask for used heels, which we used instead of rocks when playing hopscotch.

Behind the Åhmans' mansion, not far from the school, stood the Iron Works' faculty clubhouse that was not for us. A few times, however, we climbed the white picket fence and sneaked over to the special swing in the park. The swing was called "midsummer swing," for it was the type of swing that was once used during the Midsummer festivities of June 24th. It was square at the bottom for a group of people to sit or stand on while holding on to the poles that attached it to the top. On opposite sides of the square bottom we stood taking turns pumping in rhythm to get the swing going. Soon we were soaring way up past the framework—highly elated and nearly frightened to death. My mother, as a youngster, had been in a group of kids who had actually gone all the way around in the swing. I never saw anyone do that; I thought it would be extremely dangerous.

## Summers 1937-1939

Every few days at 4:00 o'clock in the afternoon, many of us met at the Iron Works' dairy with our milk cans. I remember the warmish smell of fresh milk in large vats from which our milk containers were filled by the dairy maids dressed in white from head to toe. They scooped up a liter of milk from the vat with a long-handled ladle and artfully poured it in our cans without wasting a drop. On the way home we had discovered a perfect resting place for our containers—a large, flat stump next to the path.

Ice-cream cones appeared at the Kiosk by the Post Office Bridge a few times in the summer, and word of their arrival reached all of us fast. If we had the money—if we could plead with our mothers convincingly enough—we flew there to buy one.

In the fall of 1939 when I was in third grade, I often stopped at Harjulanmäki, where Uncle Arvi lived with his wife Tyyne in the house that had belonged to Uncle Nyberg, an influential intellectual. They had a chandelier over the dining room table, a room for a maid, and store-bought rugs on the floors. Miina-Mummo now lived with them, and she was always glad to see me, letting me eat all the gooseberries I wanted from the bushes on the river bank.

Even the better homes in those days lacked conveniences taken for granted now, but my uncle's outhouse was "better" because it was private, had a rug on the floor, pictures on the wall, and ready-cut pieces of newspaper stuck to a nail.

Of all the shops in the village I knew best the Apteekki, (pharmacy), because it was the closest one, and I was allowed to run errands there. More than once I arrived only to discover that I had forgotten what it was I was supposed to buy. I was so fascinated by the rows of white medicine jars with black-rimmed labels and by the pharmacists who looked like doctors in their white frocks. I loved the smell of mixed herbs and spices, and the ringing of the cash register. We went there sometimes to buy *salmiakkia*, which, means "sal ammoniac." It came in tiny diamond-shaped black pieces in small envelopes and tasted wonderful to us—somewhat like licorice.

The general store was a co-operative in the village. Once in a great while Mother would take me there. The fragrance of ground coffee mingling with the smells of oats, raisins, rope and rubber was wonderful.

I liked entering the fabric store across the road from the co-op. The display of colorful fabrics and the feel and smell of them were much to my liking.

Open-market days were held in Värtsilä on Fridays and meant two things to us: Mother would bring us a jam-filled donut shaped like a pig, and she would buy a bagful of cinnamon rusk or zweiback that tasted great when dunked in coffee with cream.

*Chapter 4*

# Visiting Friends

**1936-1939**

My parents had many interesting friends or "places of visit," as we say in Finnish. Aunt Tyyne's parents, Herman and Maria, lived in a house that had many rather dark rooms with a cuckoo clock in each one. Since the clocks were not synchronized, they made a lot of noise all the time! Maria was from Leningrad (St. Petersburg), spoke Russian, and had exotic vases and statues, and a "samovaari" or teamaker in the dining room. She had a sunny disposition and held her hands under her apron when she talked.

The Hirvonens, Mikko and his wife, lived by the same river as Aunt Tyyne's parents. They had an extraordinary floor covering of "cork" or linoleum—yellow with bright red roses. I liked sitting on it. One day when Jöppe, my aunt, and I met Mikko on the road tipsy, he gave us each a golden 10-mark piece, which we spent at the Kiosk on chewing gum—such large amounts of it that we didn't know what to do with it. We couldn't take any home.

Mylly-täti or Aunt Mill got her name from me. She lived at the outskirts of the village in an unpainted house with one large room, the *tupa*. Somehow, coffee smelled and tasted better at her house than anywhere else. My specialty was grinding coffee beans in her coffee mill—that's where her name came from. I would do the grinding, holding the mill between my bare thighs. Every time a coffee bean got stuck in the gears, the grinder would jump and pinch my flesh. That's why I remember Mylly-täti's place so well.

Another favorite visiting place of ours was Ilmakka, the farm and home of the Leskinen brothers. There were many of them, and they reminded me of the Jukola brothers in the famous "Seven Brothers" of Aleksis Kivi. Not that they didn't know how to read or write—they were all clever—but they all were big, flaxen-haired, quiet men. Their parents had died, and only one of the brothers was married. Aino, their only sister, kept the house in good shape. Each of the young men had a specialty; one had a car and drove people around as a job on the side. Another played the *kantele*, the national stringed instrument. The Leskinens had a tractor we rode and a grindstone we were allowed to turn; Juhani especially loved to do that.

## April 1937

We had a special Easter custom in Värtsilä—and in all of Karelia— which involved the making of a colorful object called *virpoma vihta*. To make one, you needed a Y-shaped branch from a pussywillow bush, crepe paper and wire. After wrapping the branch with a strip of crepe paper, six many-layered flowers were made from the same paper, the edges curled with a knitting needle. The flowers were attached with wire along the V-part of the branch. While making this decorative object, one thought of whom the recipient should be.

On Palm Sunday the decorated branch would be brought to this chosen person, and, touching him or her gently with it, one said, "I touch you with this branch that will bring you good health and me a gift!" Then the branch was given to that person, to be reciprocated at Easter most likely with a large chocolate egg with a prize inside.

## May 1, 1937

For the first-of-May celebration of the coming of summer and *Vappu* (Labor Day), mothers would make *sima*, a cooked lemonade to which a dab of yeast gave the effect of carbonation. The brew would be bottled up and let stand in the cellar for a few days. When the raisins that had been on the bottom floated up, the brew was ready for drinking. It was delicious with fried cakes called *tippaleipä*, made of thin doughnut batter poured into boiling grease through a wax paper cone with a small hole on the tip. The result was a delightful tangle that was dusted with powdered sugar.

Dad's part in Vappu celebration was to take us to buy helium balloons or colorful pom-poms with a stick for a handle. Both were fun to swish around and to show to your friends. We would let the balloons float to the high ceiling of our staircase; there they stayed overnight. The next morning we took them down and played with them until they lost their helium and shriveled up.

## June 24, 1938

Juhannus, the Midsummer festival on the 24th of June was the celebration of the longest day of the year. Finland's flag would fly all through the night, for the sun would not set. Dad would get two young birch trees and place them on both sides of our front door. He would bring home a whole crate of soda bottles with white ceramic corks. Red raspberry was my favorite. It painted my lips red.

On Juhannus the new sports center, Kisapirtti, was the place for organized activities. Besides the bands, we had fireworks, dancing, choirs singing, and the *kokko* or bonfire. Nowhere had I seen so many people or so many things, or heard more noise, than at Kisapirtti. The highlight was a piece of cake or *leivos*, a pink-topped delight of flavor.

At Kisapirtti movies were shown throughout the year. There I saw my first movie, *Meren urhot* or *The Old Man and the Sea* with Spencer Tracy. I remember the sadness after he died in the sea, and a wreath of flowers was thrown in the water from the ship. At Kisapirtti I also danced my first folkdance, *Kalliolle, kukkulalle*, in a huge circle.

## February 1937

Once every winter, my dad rented a horse and sleigh from the Iron Works' stables, and we rode to the Heiskanens' home ten kilometers away. It was fun to sit under the covers and stare at the horse's behind—and especially at his tail, which once in a while rose, driving us squealing under the covers! Coming back from the Heiskanens was more fun because the horse would run without Dad's encouragement, wanting to get back to his stable and knew the way, which made me feel safer. Although Dad had been a farm boy, I don't think he knew much about horses.

One winter of deep snow, we built a large snow castle in our front yard. Together we rolled the snow into huge balls that took two to carry, made a circle of them and added layers until it looked like a castle. Here and there we left an opening for a window and, at ground level, for a door. At dusk we lit candles in the windows, and during the day we played with water colored by soaking different colored crepe paper in it. We poured the tinted water into bottles and placed them in the castle's windows. We continually added refinements—furniture made of snow or a supply of snowballs to guard against enemy attack. After a freezing night the castle was strong and solid until either a snowball fight or a thaw brought it down.

## June-August 1936-1939

We never had any pets while in Värtsilä, but a cat was part of my early life. Seppo, a tiger-colored cat belonged to a neighbor. I liked to carry him around and, once in a while, had permission to bring him upstairs to our home. I fed him milk and watched him licking his lips afterwards. Since then I have loved cats.

A colorful addition to our daily lives in Värtsilä was Crazy Herman, as we called him. He passed by our house herding his cows with a long, thin pole, calling each by name. They were names of different kinds of berries—Mustikka and Mansikka (Blueberry and Strawberry)—or Hertta and Heluna. He often kicked stones from under his cows' feet, as if to make it more comfortable for them to walk. By doing so, he raised a cloud of light dust that settled in layers over the tall weeds with yellow button-like flowers that grew on the edges of the ditch.

## April 1937

Doctor Adolf Wasenius was the busy, competent chief surgeon of the Värtsilä Hospital, who took care of all ailments. One spring I had a painful ear infection that he cured by putting a few ice-cold drops in my ear. That was the end of that malady, and I respected him from that moment on, even if I was afraid of him. He was dark, cross-eyed, and hairy—even on his fingers. People said they often were cured in the waiting room before even seeing him, just because they were so afraid of him!

The Ladies of Sortavala were peddlers who came from time to time to our yard to sell their wares. They had large two-story suitcases with hinges, with things from thimbles and mirrors to pants and coats. Once I tried on a blue cloak that spread out nicely when I spun around. Another time I tried on a plaid dress with a full skirt that I liked a lot. I didn't get either garment, but I did get an idea: I talked my mother into ordering red velvet for a full-skirted dress for me.

Chapter 5

# The Winter War, 1939-1940

## July-November 1935

Sad events occurred even before the war. Once when at the lake, we received word that our next-door neighbor, Seile, had shot himself, just on the other side of our living room wall. We got new neighbors, the Skutnabbs, whose son Jorma became ill with tuberculosis and later died of it. Another young man of seventeen was accidentally shot while hunting. My Aunt Anni's third child was born too soon and died in a few days. I remember him in an open coffin in the hallway, and how his three-year-old brother Reijo said, "Seppo Tapani" (his name), while touching his dead brother's head. A man by the name of Uuno lost his foot to gangrene, and our Uncle Arvi was sent to a sanitarium for tuberculosis. The day he left, Juhani and I, watching him from the living room window, cried. He waved to us as he slowly walked to the gate, a suitcase in his hand. Pulmonary tuberculosis was widely spread in those days and most of the time led to death, but after many months Uncle Arvi returned home, recovered.

## March 1939

Although as second graders we had been making gas masks at school, we didn't really comprehend the gravity of the situation in Finland in 1939. The masks were face-sized cushions made of white flannel and charcoal, and were attached around our little heads with elastic bands.

## June 1939

The first hint of war came to me at the age of eight, listening to conversations of grown-ups. Germany was at war, and the fighting was getting closer. I remember thinking that war couldn't happen to us because, for one thing, I had not yet received the velvet fabric we had ordered from the Sortavala Ladies, and, for another, America would help us—America, the large, rich country across the ocean. When it was daytime here, it was nighttime there. I had met some visitors from America in the village and had heard that.

## August 1939

Increasing signs of war: the rumble of heavy equipment on the road at night, the army reserves long since called in, and young men being drafted. When we observed that a lot of woodpeckers had stationed themselves in the trees by our homes, many believed it to be an omen of war. Everyone knew that woodpeckers normally stayed in the woods.

## September 1939

Finally, the parcel from the Ladies of Sortavala arrived, but it contained some red corduroy material instead of velvet and not nearly enough for a full skirt. I was terribly disappointed. The schools soon closed their doors, and children started a project of digging dugouts on the field by the edge of the woods. We collected materials to keep out the rain and installed fireplaces with stovepipes in them. There we spent many evenings by the fire roasting potatoes, which tasted simply delicious.

## September 1939

Then one day, everybody stopped what they were doing to watch a parade—hundreds of Värtsilä's young men turned soldiers, marching proudly to the music of the Firemen's Band, singing patriotic songs as they passed our gate. "When one's homeland is in danger, we must go to war . . ." said one song. "It's beautiful to die fighting for your country when you are young, dying the death of a hero . . ." said another, and "Oh, dearest Finland, let me listen to the roar of your rapids and to the murmur of your pines until the moment of my departure comes. . . . One needs only the honor of hearing from one's tomb the whispering of your fir trees when you (motherland) have covered up your son for his final rest. . . ."

We knew then that war was imminent. We stood at the fence with heavy hearts, weeping for our boys and for Finland.

## October 1939

The first air raid alarm sounded when Juhani, Anja and I were alone. Mother had gone marketing. Fortunately she was turned back by an officer who told her that enemy planes had crossed Finland's border, and that an alarm would sound any minute. When I heard the siren, I grabbed Anja who was three and asleep, and started dragging her toward the stairway. Juhani ran before me. We met Mother downstairs, and together we ran to the woods in a crazy tangle of people. Later we came to realize that the army fuel and ammunition depot was in the woods. We subsequently chose a potato cellar across the road by the Rectory as our shelter.

When the frequency of the alarms increased, Mother decided to take us away to the countryside, away, at least from the sound of the sirens. One farmhouse where we stayed was cold and dank, and the family had a sick child. We eventually returned home only to have the brightness of the electric lights hurt eyes accustomed to the light of flickering storm lanterns. Everywhere we stayed I crocheted dust clothes—round and square ones made of white cotton yarn with colorful fringes around them. As we left each family, I gave them a dust cloth as a little thank-you.

## December 1939

In the middle of December 1939, the official evacuation of women and children took place. All I remember of the night we left our home forever was pitch blackness full of the muffled urgency of many families like ours. My father pushed the chair sled loaded with our essentials. We walked in silence. At the dimly lit station, we were escorted to the train, where we said our goodbyes to Dad, who stayed behind.

The first train was a comfortable passenger train where some friendly Army nurses served us milk and hardtack sandwiches. All that mattered after that was the consoling feeling of getting away from the war, and I soon fell asleep. When I awoke, the train was being emptied; we had to change trains. Half asleep I remember dragging the mattress-sack full of possessions, my responsibility for, at eight, I was the oldest child of our family.

The second train was not very comfortable, composed of cattle cars with modified loft-like shelves for people, and one small window. In our car a Franklin-type stove in the middle helped a little. A lot more people had joined us by then. It was cold, and some children cried. Daylight brought the danger of the train being seen from the air by enemy planes. We knew the enemy wanted to cut off all supply and communication lines to the front. They often bombed important railroad junctions. And, since a dark train posed a visible target in the middle of the snowy fields, every time an alarm sounded, we leaped out of the car into the snow and covered ourselves up in it. We were lucky; the planes that flew over us that day did not drop bombs. Perhaps they were just making maps.

At one point during our trip, Mother decided to change our travel plans. She had sized up the situation and decided that instead of evacuating with the multitude of people, we would change trains and head for Massilanmäki, west of Savonlinna, where we had relatives. She inquired and begged the officers and soldiers to allow us to do that. I was relieved. I had agonized about getting lost in the multitude with my big bag. Mother had found a solution. We would board on a military train going west. With my mattress-sack in tow, I frantically followed mother, who carried Anja and a suitcase while pulling Juhani along. We pushed and were pushed, but at the end of our struggle, we found ourselves comfortably accommodated in the compartment of kind military officers. One of them let me sleep in his lamb-fur coat. All was well.

We arrived safely at our relatives' farmhouse at Massilanmäki. In bed after taking a sauna that night, I was all ears, intrigued by the conversation Aunt Hanna and Mother were having about Free-Masons and eerie cemeteries. The next day, however, we received the shocking news that the very train we had ridden had been bombed. The entire train was lost and everybody on it dead. The enemy had bombed a civilian train. In our grief we were thankful for Mother's decision to change trains.

When we left Värtsilä, we also left behind my dad, who, with many others who worked at the Iron Works, had stayed to prepare it for evacuation. Dad's letters told of the flood of refugees coming from the east with their cattle and belongings. He told of the damage done by the many bombings in Värtsilä and of the numbers of fallen soldiers, one of them Jukka Hallasalo, whom I had always admired. Nanna Käki's young husband, Jukka had marched among the soldiers singing about the honor of dying for one's homeland, not long before.

In one of his letters Dad told us of the bravery of a special young woman, seventeen years of age, who had volunteered to stay and care for the dead. The frozen corpses were brought to the Factory's drying barn, which was used as the morgue. With the help of an older man, she sorted and labeled the frozen bodies, placing them in coffins for shipping home. Värtsilä was a primary center for supplies to the front and also served to nurse the wounded. Hundreds of prisoners of war were cared for there.

## Chapter 6

# Evacuees in Savo

**December 1939-March 1940**

Massilanmäki, the destination of our flight from the war, was a community of medium-sized farms in Savo, a province in Finland just west of Karelia. A major railway, running east to west, passed through the community.

The little Massilanmäki station housed the telegraph and telephone systems and received mail every morning. Twenty kilometers west was Savonlinna, the closest city. Five kilometers away was Kallislahti, a fair-sized village where most people did their shopping. My family had visited Massilanmäki in the summer of 1936 when my sister Anja was just one week old.

The head of the family with which we stayed was a farmer named Antti Massinen, whose wife Hanna was my Miina-Mummo's half sister. Aunt Hanna ran her household efficiently and worked hard at everything from milking the cows to baking large amounts of rye bread weekly. An expert midwife for humans and animals alike, she knew remedies for most ailments of both.

Aunt Hanna was different from most farmers' wives in that she wasn't tied to her work, but would at times take a vacation. Suddenly she just announced that she was going to visit so and so, trusting that someone would do her work.

Antti, Hanna's husband, was the opposite; large, quiet and slow-moving, he was content as long as he had his horse to work with, his sauna, his rye bread, and his buttermilk. He was very interested in the war news, especially in the demands the government placed on his household—his quotas of kilos of meat or cheese and liters of milk needed for the war effort.

Antti wore a cup-like eyeglass attached with a black elastic band around his head. He wore a puukko-knife on his belt, and used it for cutting bread and meat into bite-sized pieces, which he brought to his mouth between his thumb and the blade. After eating he wanted to hear the latest news from anyone who had read the daily paper or had heard from a neighbor.

To help out, I sometimes milked a cow. I churned butter in a tall, wooden churn by moving the stick up and down. Later we used a metal churn that rotated horizontally. I would peek in to see little clots of butter bouncing on the milk. When enough butter clumped up, it was removed from the churn with a wooden spatula. The remaining milk had become *kirnupiimä* or buttermilk and was tasty.

I also learned to comb wool, "carding" it between two wide brushes with hundreds of needle-sized spikes. I brushed the lump of wool between the two brushes until nice and fluffy. Then I piled these fluffs in a basket, ready for spinning.

Spinning is not the easiest of skills to learn; one had to attend to many things at the same time: pumping with the right foot, working the combed fluff of wool, controlling the wheel and watching the yarn feed through the spinner and onto the spindle.

The daily event I liked best was skiing down to the station to pick up the mail for the Massinen household. When the mail delivery came, the station chief read off the names on the mail. I always looked for a letter from Dad. Many evenings Mother and I walked on crunchy snow to our neighbors to listen to the radio news.

## January 1940

As children, we were thrilled as well as frightened by the talk about spies. We were told that they were eager for news and even tapped telephone lines to pick it up. Then they reported it to the enemy. On the walls of the railway stop, on poles and on store fronts, posters warned us of spies. We were to keep our mouths shut, our ears and eyes open, for it was hard to tell who might be a spy!

## February 1940

Once my father came to Massilanmäki for a short visit. I remember the night Mother and I took him back to Kallislahti, five kilometers away, carrying his luggage on a chair sled. He returned to Värtsilä where the Iron Works still operated.

Feeling sad, Mother and I took our leave of him and started our journey back. The night was starless, the woods on both sides of the road very black, and the wind sighed through the trees and howled in the telephone lines. The weather had recently eased, and the thaw made the chair sled run easily. Suddenly, Mother touched my head from behind and whispered to keep down. She had heard something in the woods. Branches snapped, and we could hear barely-audible voices. Spies! Mother kicked harder to make the sled run faster. We said nothing the rest of the way but were glad to reach a clearing and see the friendly light of houses.

Often at night we blew out our lantern and stood by the corner of the house watching orange-colored oval objects move back and forth in the sky above the woods. This sighting told us that Savonlinna, the closest city, would be bombed next morning. If during the day an airplane flew the same route—back and forth, back and forth—over the woods, the following night Savonlinna again suffered a bombing raid.

We had been instructed to lie down and roll in the snow if caught in the open, away from any structures when we heard a bomber. One day that happened to Juhani, who was out skiing by himself. From the tupa window we could see him, a black spot on the white field near the woods, when we heard the bomber.

Nothing happened to Juhani, but when we asked him what he had done, he said he did what he was supposed to do, except that since the snow wouldn't stick to his clothes, he had lain on his back and watched the red star under the bomber's belly pass over him.

At Massilanmäki: Left: Manu, his children, Aunt Hanna, 1949.

*Chapter 7*

# The Smoke Sauna and the Refugees

## January 1940

Once I did some spying on my own, but on Aulis, the fifteen-year-old son of the Massinens, and a friend of his. They were secretly smoking home-grown tobacco called *kessu*. From a window of the tupa facing the barn, if I flattened my face sideways against the glass, I could see the corner of the house where the two boys rolled kessu in pieces of paper. They lighted them, inhaled smoke, then choked and coughed. When I told them that I knew their secret, they threatened to give me a good spanking if I ever told any-one, but I saw their distress. I enjoyed being in a position of power.

Sometimes I rolled my hair in curlers made of willow. Impi, one of the Massinens' daughters used them. Together we cut up an old inner tube into rubber bands to hold the curlers in place. I wanted the boys to notice my curls.

On Saturday evenings the smoke sauna was prepared for everyone. An old ritual, considered medicine for many ills, the smoke sauna was meant to purify the body inside and out. It was calming too, the highlight of the week. The Massinens' sauna was old, without a chimney and so flimsy that the smoke poured out through the cracks in the walls. Heated by a fire in the fireplace, which was not much more than a pile of rocks onto which a huge kettle was placed for heating water at the same time, everything inside was sooty: the platform, the benches, the walls, and the ceiling. On the floor stood a large barrel of cold water. On the bench were individual basins, sponges and soap for washing. Hairpins and such were placed on the sooty window sill.

The men usually went for their bath first because they supposedly could stand more heat. After entering the sauna, one removed all clothes and climbed up to a seat on the bench on the platform. Whenever every-body agreed to be ready, a dipperful of water was thrown on the hot rocks of the fireplace, and a great amount of steam was produced. One dipped a birch switch in a bucket of warm water and started gently touching the legs and arms with it. Immediately a wonderful aroma of fresh birch filled the sauna, making one want more steam, and perhaps more "beating" with the switch. Some liked it hotter than others; one also could go lower or outside to cool off. In the winter some went out and rolled in the snow; in the summer, if the sauna happened to be on a lake, a swim felt good.

Scrubbing took place next; each one scrubbing someone else. When finished and wrapped in a towel, it was time to walk back to the house and get dressed. At the tupa table, "silver tea" or hot water with milk was served with something freshly baked. During the war that was the custom; in better times coffee and beer were available. Saturday was thus complete. One felt clean, refreshed and brand-new and part of the whole circle of people.

The rationing of food and other items became a part of life from the start of the war. Coffee was the most missed item for the grown-ups. "Replacement coffee" was made of ground up dandelion roots toasted in a coffee roaster. By no means the same as real coffee, at least the "coffee" gave you a break in your routine. Our half a pound of sugar per person per month did not come in granulated form but in big, hard cones that Mother cut up into irregular, sharp pieces with a special scissors.

Perhaps the most obvious sign of war at Massilanmäki was seen in the trains that passed us, puffing up the hill in a cloud of steam, day and night. As they approached our stop, they blew their whistle, and, from the type of whistling sound, we could tell if the train would stop or not. Trains coming from the east had some cars painted white with large red crosses over the sides and the roofs. They brought back the seriously wounded. An agreement between nations prohibited the bombing of trains painted in such a way. Most of the trains coming from the war also had cars marked with fir trees; they contained the corpses.

In January 1940 when I had my ninth birthday, the flow of refugees my father had mentioned flocking to Värtsilä, reached us in Massilanmäki. Thousands came! The local authorities knew how many people each household could handle, and assigned them accordingly. Our first group arrived after dark. They had traveled hundreds of kilometers, walking or taking turns riding in the sleighs pulled by exhausted horses. They carried meager possessions. Many even drove their cattle. Cows and horses had frozen to death on the way, and those that remained were in bad shape.

Among the first wave of refugees were the Nisonens, a big man and a small woman who was Aunt Hanna's other half sister. They came from east of Värtsilä where they had a farm I remembered visiting. They had lost everything but a horse and a few belongings in the sleigh. The woman sobbed often. When finally we went to bed, no space at all remained on the tupa floor; every spot was taken up by a very tired person.

When not sobbing, Mrs. Nisonen seemed all action. First she called for huge kettles of water to be heated for the animals. And all animals had to be placed in the barn or stable; after the trek they would not last another below-freezing night. She delivered a calf that first night in the barn. One of those miracles one hears about happened to her—her brown hair turned gray overnight!

I listened to the refugees' stories about their dying animals and burning houses, artillery charges, and people who refused to leave their homes. The story I remember best concerned a woman refugee who turned out to be a male spy. He had been discovered when he scratched the stubble of his beard at night.

The flood of refugees continued. As soon as one group felt able, they left us to continue their journey west to a designated community. New refugees took their place. Captured Russian soldiers were accommodated in some farm houses and made to work. They wore long, gray mantles of the Finnish Army, and funny knit caps with a "horn" on the crown. Their help was needed; most able-bodied men had been drafted.

Aunt Linda arrived by her own means to live with the Luukkainens some distance away. At times we walked to where she stayed to have a "decent" sauna—not a smoky one—with her. One of Luukkainen's daughters was a *lotta*, an Army nurse. She looked splendid in her gray uniform with Army insignia on her high-collared labels. To me she was a symbol of patriotism.

In early March, in addition to the temporary refugees, many of our relatives suddenly appeared at the Massinens' farm house: Miina-Mummo, Aunt Tyyne, her parents, and her baby son. There were fourteen of us living in two bedrooms and the tupa. Plus the refugees!

## March 25, 1940

Perhaps it was the confusion of so many people under one roof that made my mother decide to move us on. Or perhaps it was because in March 1940 the war ended, and Värtsilä was lost to the Soviet Union. One day we picked up our things, boarded a train going west, and, after several hundred kilometers, arrived at Virrat, where most of the Värtsilä evacuees had been relocated. Among them were Mother's mother Mamma, my four aunts, and Aunt Anni's children, Reijo and Pirkko. At Virrat we felt right at home. Since Värtsilä had been handed over to the Russians, everybody had left, including my father.

*Chapter 8*

# At Virrat

**March 25-27, 1940**

Our long train trip across Finland ended at a stop called Koronkylä, near Virrat, the main village. There were eight of us: Mother, Juhani, Anja, and I of our family, plus Aunt Tyyne (Uncle Arvi's wife) with her infant son and her parents. They had begged Mother not to leave them as we departed Massilanmäki. At Virrat, Mother immediately found her way to the housing authorities, and soon a place was found for us. A vacated co-op bank building on the main road, the place even had a telephone. Our family soon took over the right side of the building, and Aunt Tyyne's group took the left side.

Virrat and Koronkylä were in the province of Häme on the shores of Lake Näsijärvi, the largest lake in the lake system by the same name. In the middle of Finland, in the region of large farms and well-to-do farmers, the people of Häme were said to be quiet and uncommunicative, and spoke a dialect of Finnish all their own. It was peaceful at Koronkylä, and there was plenty of food. It seemed as if the war had not even touched them. Typically of Häme, the farms were named Ylä-Patala and Ala-Patala, meaning Upper and Lower Patala. The farm houses were huge with enormous tupas that had unpainted, well-scrubbed floors, huge ovens and often a loom in the corner. It was customary in Häme to bake large quantities of round, flat, rye breads with a hole in the middle and hang them by the holes on horizontal poles running across one part of the high ceiling of the tupa. The bread dried up, but stayed very delicious. The milk, yogurt, cream and butter were unrationed. The granaries and storehouses had two stories, decorated with wood carvings at the front. And they were full of food!

The only evidence that war had touched life in Häme was that no young men remained in the village; the farms were run by older men and young boys. Since it was winter, their work consisted of taking care of the animals and, in their spare time activities whittling and carving tool handles. No trees were felled, for not many forests grew in Häme, unlike the country around Savo and Karelia.

After the ice melted on Lake Näsijärvi and signs of spring filled the air, Mother started talking about moving to Helsinki, the capital. Dad had gone there to the shipyard owned by the same Värtsilä Concern he had always worked for. On his visit, he had told Mother that as soon as he found a place for us to live, he would send for us.

## May 1940

When Dad reported that he had found an apartment, only six months had passed since we left Värtsilä. To me it seemed a much longer time. We had seen and learned so much; how hard it must have been for the grown-ups! Children didn't understand things the same way they did, and we didn't worry about the next day, even less about our futures. In six months we had switched from the dialect of Karelia to that of Savo. The Häme dialect didn't "take," however, for we lived among Karelians. But I had mastered the Savo dialect—even bragged about it to amuse those around me. My favorite sentence in the Savo dialect had to do with it being so cold outside that even my eyebrows hurt: "On niin juloman kylömä ilema, että silemäkulomia kylömää," which has six extra vowels added to standard Finnish. Now we headed toward Helsinki with its famous slang.

*Chapter 9*

# Helsinki

**June 1940**

My first peek at our apartment on the second floor at Vallininkuja gave me a good feeling, for the living room looked spacious without any furniture. It had a white-tiled stove-oven at the corner. Two windows faced the street, and the sun shone in. The kitchen had running water.

The long, gray building was made of stuccoed wood in the 1920s style. It had two stories, a few bay windows and stretched over three streets like a fortress. It even had a turret at its highest point. With another building, it formed an enclosure with a yard. The dozen entrances, marked from A to L, opened onto the yard, housing four to six apartments each. A sidewalk led from the main gate to the entrances on the left and right. The gate, made of iron bars, was locked at 9:00 PM each night by the custodian. Entrance "F" had two real toilets for its residents. The rest of us had to contend with outhouses.

In June 1940 my family arrived in Helsinki; a half year earlier we had been tending our lives in Värtsilä, Karelia. Then the war made us evacuees—400,000 of us altogether. We were glad we had a place we could call home again, for an acute housing shortage due to the loss of Karelia to the Russians had made many homeless. It didn't matter to us that we ate from the top of our suitcase and slept on the floor.

Then one day our furniture arrived. The *piironki* or chest-of-drawers, with its blue glass doors, came all wrapped up in rugs, unharmed, its drawers containing many useful things. The pink *Ha Taurmo* lamp arrived as did the alarm clock. One delicate Japanese tea cup with green, hand-painted parrots had survived a bombing and the trip; the rest of the dishes hadn't. Our table, some chairs, and the trundle beds arrived also. Pretty soon we felt well equipped.

Our kitchen was fairly small, dark and cold in the winter. The view from its window was of the garbage bins and the outhouses. But a sink with running water! I enjoyed washing dishes for a while because of that.

At that point my family consisted of five members: Dad, Mother, Juhani—seven, Anja—four, and me—nine. We were the largest family in the housing complex of about two hundred people. Most were steady workers who accepted their fate and obediently went about their daily business. In addition to Dad, two other men worked for the Värtsilä Concern in Helsinki.

It didn't take me long to get acquainted with other kids who lived in the same building. There were a dozen of them, and I'm still in touch with five: Inge, Magi, Bisse, Laila and Nita. We played games, performed plays, went swimming and skiing and learned the facts of life from the older girls.

Of the grown-ups, Manda was a colorful character with her water-wrinkled hands (she was a professional washer woman) and toothless mouth that spoke a mixture of Swedish and Finnish. "The Knitter" was another character; she was funny all the time. From birth she had short, crippled legs which she covered up with long skirts. Short and stocky, her most prominent feature was her large bosom that covered the upper half of her. I was thankful to her for the undershirts she knitted for me; I needed them being allergic to wool.

Seven families had Swedish as a native tongue. In my family only my mother spoke it with Mamma. We all understood everything, though. The worst speaker of Finnish was the owner of the property; I saw him once a month when paying the rent. He had thin, fluffy white hair, and he kept his small glasses half way down his nose. He sat hunched over, mumbling to himself in Swedish while scribbling numbers in his big book—like Scrooge himself.

Keijo Komppa, a dandyish young man, I seem to remember with a white student cap on his head. He lived with his gentle mother, and sang opera-style at their open window daily. We imitated him a lot, making fun of him, no doubt. Keijo, however, became a well-known singer and an accomplished actor for the National Theater in Helsinki.

Our first year in Helsinki was a time of peace in Finland. But everything was still rationed, and one lived within the limits of "coupons," designated for specific items. For instance, a child's allotment was six deciliters (approximately three cups) of milk a day; the grown-ups got half as much. The clerks at the milk and bread stores had a pair of scissors attached with string to their belts for cutting out coupons for so much milk and so many loaves of white or dark bread.

Families had to plan out an entire month so as not to end up without food. Potatoes, the main staple, were not rationed but not plentiful either. Every time word reached us about potatoes being sold at a store, Juhani and I were sent there to stand in line. Many times we stood in line for an hour or two, and sometimes the potatoes we got were frost-bitten and tasted bad.

The time came when we resorted to paper bed sheets, which rattled and felt like crepe paper against us, but were warm and became more comfortable with use. Whatever could be reused in some other form, was used. Mother's summer coat became a dress for me that never wore out, but made me sigh every time I had to wear it. At first our shoes had leather uppers and wooden soles—clogs—but gradually the upper became paper fiber with soles of plywood. That made them bendable—and more comfortable.

The sugar allotment was a half pound per person per month. Once my brother Juhani ate his entire ration at one sitting while the rest of us watched him with admiration and horror. One time we played Monopoly for six hours at my friend Pirkko's house and got so hungry we begged to borrow a piece of rye bread from her family. The next day we each paid back our share.

## January 1941-1942

One of the government mandates was that each family had to cut a certain number of cubic meters of wood for the common good. Since my father was the only one in the family capable of doing that, every time he returned from the woods, we were eager to help his aching back by massaging him. He flopped on the floor and the three of us crawled on our hands and knees all over his back and legs and, according to his grunts and instructions, massaged every muscle in his body from head to toe. He loved that!

## May 1942

One way the school children helped the country was by going to the countryside to cut large amounts of willow branches. We cut piles and piles of them, then peeled the skin off them, stuffed the peels into potato sacks and transported them to the city. The willow peels were used for shoe making. We also collected scrap metal, bottles and paper for the common good.

Chapter 10

# Elementary School Times
# 1940-1943

The schools in Helsinki filled to overflowing with the Karelian refugee children, and new facilities had to be opened up to accommodate all. I ended up at Työväen Opisto Learning Center, in fourth grade, although I hadn't attended third grade for more than two weeks a year earlier in Värtsilä.

The teacher who influenced me most of all of my teachers was Elsa Vartiainen, my fifth and sixth grade teacher. About sixty, tall, slender, unmarried, and very much a patriot, Miss Vartiainen, too, was a refugee, from Viipuri, Karelia, not very far from where I came from. She tied her graying, thin hair tightly on a bun on top of her head, but a few wispy curls on both sides of her face softened her looks. Many small wrinkles filled her fragile face, but her voice was authoritative, as was the sound of her heels as she entered the classroom. She wore a dark blue dress with a high collar held together in front by a Kalevala brooch.

Daily out of her metal lunch box came a heel-sized rye-bread sandwich with potato puree between the slices. She picked up the tiny sandwich carefully, daintily holding it as she bit into it with reverence. She reminded us of the times in which we lived, how we had to sacrifice our comfort and to do our share for our country. We needed to be neat and thrifty. She told us how she hung her dresses from her window to ventilate them. That way they didn't need washing as often and would last longer—and so help the country. The food we were allotted with coupons was sufficient, she said, and would keep us healthy. Brisk exercise in fresh air was essential for our well-being. No matter how cold it was outside. Once an hour we opened the classroom windows for ventilation, and every hour we bundled up and descended four stories for a recess outside. We took our liquid vitamin dosage on a tiny piece of bread in the classroom. We learned not to drop anything on the floor and to pick up after others, when necessary.

Every noon my class walked to a nearby elementary school where hot

lunch was served. It was either watery beef-vegetable soup or a thin por-
ridge of rye flour, called "sawdust meal." Twice a week we walked to the
same school for gym. There, after warm-ups and floor exercises, our teacher
instructed us—for instance, on how to set our feet, knees, and hands for
climbing the ropes. Effortlessly and gracefully she reached the ceiling with
a few calculated stretchings and pulls, and while wearing her narrow dark
blue wool dress and in her heels. I never made it to the ceiling, and every
stretch and pull was less than effortless for me. But I was good with the
"horses," and in high jump, and I could easily do the splits. The floor exercises on the bare wooden floor, on the other hand, were painful on my
skinny back. I was a fairly good runner and skier, but not good in basket-
ball.

From Elsa Vartiainen we learned about Finland's heroes, of its lakes
and its green gold, the forests. We knew Finland's needs, and who its enemy
was. We learned to knit woollen socks with five needles—the heel was the
trickiest part. Every time we had a run-away stitch, we lined up with our
knitting to ask for our teacher's help. We learned hundreds of songs from
hymns to ballads, some in two voices. We acted out plays; "Not Everyone
Is Equally Lucky" was one for Christmas.

## February 1943

In sixth grade we took a field trip on a bus to Porvoo, an old historical
town about fifty kilometers east of Helsinki. We visited the cemetery
where many of the heroes we had learned about lay buried. We visited a
school for the deaf and blind. At lunch time, we ate in a cafe, handling our
own money. No wonder I still remember how exciting the trip was.

In Miss Vartianen's class I met Pirkko Viljanen, who became a life-long
friend. She and I competed for a scholarship for two years; Pirkko got it in
the fifth year, I in the sixth.

## March 1943

For a winter sport, we skated on the rink across the street from our
school. There I worked on my second great wish, that of becoming a figure
skater. (The first wish was a red velvet dress.) I watched the lucky girls who
had white figure skates and white stockings under skimpy velvet costumes.
I practiced figure eights, jumps and pirouettes after school and in the evenings on my too-large hockey skates. I loved to watch skating competitions
wherever they were held in town. When I was ready, I invited my father
to observe me. He came and was convinced that I deserved a proper pair
of skates. Since there were no skates for sale in the stores, we turned to
newspaper ads, and on Sunday mornings took a street car to addresses that
had figure skates for sale. Each time, however, we came too late; the skates
had been already sold. So I never got my second great wish, either.

Chapter 11

# The War Continues

In July 1941, the war between Finland and Soviet Union started anew, meaning less food, fewer clothes, air raid alarms that interrupted our sleep, and bombs. War also meant covering your windows tightly at night. No light was allowed to escape in hopes of fooling the enemy about the location of Helsinki. Authorized people patrolled the streets, penalizing people if windows were not properly covered. During that summer when I was ten, our doll playing was often disrupted by air raid sirens, which meant enemy bombers were coming. We ran for shelter. Most of the time we ran to "4," the basement of the four-story apartment building across the street, which was a shelter against bomb fragments only, not against bombs. It had been reinforced with sacks of sand and heavy beams of wood, like a bunker. There were benches to sit on and a loft for the kids.

After an all-clear signal had sounded during the day, we would return to our dolls, only this time the play consisted of "alarms," "shelters," and "bombings." We then ran with our dolls.

I always read the headlines in the *Helsingin Sanomat*, such as "Kollaa kestää!" or "Kollaa holds on!" and listened to the radio news with my parents. Many battles against the enemy were won, some were lost. I knew Värtsilä had been won back on the first day of the "Continuation War," as it was called. Many people returned there, but we never considered that. Värtsilä was in bad shape; most of its wooden structures had burned down, and even the Iron Works itself had been damaged in a bombing. Someone who visited there told us that the metal roofing of our summer cottage had been torn off and buckets made of it.

Every Thursday evening I listened to "Markus setä" or Uncle Marcus," a children's radio program. Radio plays were another interest of our family; "Sonny Boy" was memorable for its sadness. The song said something about the betrayal of friends, and "You are the dearest to me, Sonny Boy!" On Saturday evenings I enjoyed listening to both classical and popular music on the radio—as requested by people who called in. Some Sunday afternoons a group of us went to the matinees in a theater on Helsinki Street. Often we saw a Shirley Temple film, and I admired her looks, her dancing and singing. Once we saw the movie about the guillotine death of Marie Antoinette and her husband Louie. While watching the dreadful happenings on the screen, we anxiously ate hard peas in place of candy.

My girlfriends and I liked to take babies for strolls in carriages. We knew who had babies and what kinds of buggies; the newer and fancier the buggy was, the better. We knocked on a door, asking the mother if she wanted her baby to have an outing. Often we got our wish. I particularly liked taking my cousin Marjatta, Aunt Anni's baby, for a stroll for she was good-natured, looked pretty in her yellow coat, and had cute dimples. Her buggy was new, dark blue and had wonderful, big wheels and bouncing springs. She and her family, the Bambergs, lived close to us. Mother's mother Mamma and her daughters Viola and Hjördis lived with the Bambergs. Their home was in a new building with gas stoves, for which they purchased "tokens" to insert into the gas meter. They had a bathtub and hot water, although in limited quantities and only on certain days. Sometimes Mamma invited me over for a bath. Aunt Anni and her husband Pauli both worked for the Värtsilä Concern, and Mamma took care of the children.

## August 1942

Brother Pentti and my cousin Raimo were born during a bombing, which meant that Mother and Anni were quickly released from the hospital. Because of Pentti, we received a CARE package from America. All babies born at that time received one. Among other things the package contained Jello. We didn't know what it was but we licked the tasty powder. There was meat from Argentina under the label of "Spam," and a can of shortening, smooth as silk. I used it for skin lotion.

Since my childhood I had had problems with my skin. Where it itched, I scratched, often during the night without knowing it, often dreaming of doing some heroic deed—until I was bloody at the ankles, elbows and knees. Then the bandages would get stuck to the ooze and dried before morning. For tens of years, I suffered with this, making it hard to face the mornings.

When an infection hit, I would soak my feet in hot water, spread Ichtammol salve on them, then wrap them in bandages, take aspirin for the ache and fever, and suffer in bed until it passed.

## June 1943

My friends and I no longer played with dolls, and those of us who were at least twelve (and I was) went to work. I got a job at a flower shop in the center of Helsinki, delivering flowers all over the city. I traveled by street car with a monthly pass and got to know the entire city quite well. I also learned something about flower arrangements, funeral wreaths, and sprays. Often my job started when the shop closed for the day. I hung five to six wrapped-up deliveries on the fingers of my left hand in the order of destinations, planning my "rounds."

Having finished sixth grade and won a scholarship, during the summer of 1943 I took the entrance exam to the Third Finnish Girls' School, a government-supported school in an old part of the city. Many of us gathered at the front door and on the stairs leading up to the inner door, waiting to hear the announcement read with the names of those who had passed the exam. Both Pirkko and I passed and were most happy.

## September 1943

For the first time, I was shopping for new books and supplies at bookstores, ready to attend secondary school. I would have a different teacher for each subject and study a foreign language, Swedish. But school had barely started when the air raid alarms grew constant, and we ended up spending our nights in a shelter. Often several alarms sounded in one night. If an alarm lasted past ten o'clock PM, we would have no classes the next day.

## February 1944

Leave it to the kids; we actually were curious to go around our part of Helsinki after a bombing, to see which buildings had been wiped out. Often after a bombing, we picked up ammunition fragments from our backyard. One day, the school where we went for physical examinations was hit—we rejoiced!

It was my responsibility to look after my brother Juhani, who was nine, during the alarms. Mother had Anja and Pentti to watch, and Dad dashed out to fulfill the duties assigned to him. Juhani was hard to wake up and slow to get going; we were always the last ones out.

One night no one was out but us. Heavy bombers filled the sky between the buildings. We could hear the popping of machine gun fire around us, and the heavy rumble of the planes echoing from the walls. We could tell they were flying low. Anti-aircraft artillery, situated on the camouflaged Water Castle, shot at the planes. I pulled Juhani along by his hand as we continued our journey, crouching and hugging the walls as we went, toward the real bomb shelter inside solid granite bedrock. As we crossed the street, all hunched up, a policeman on horseback reached us, jumped off his horse and rushed us toward the nearest building. He then kicked in a cellar window and made us crawl in. We were to stay there until the all-clear siren sounded.

We were safe, and Mother only learned about our adventure when it was over. We were scolded for not having run to "4," the fragment shelter, which was much closer. However, I was only following the rule we had about alarms: we alternated between the two places, and this time it was the real bomb shelter's turn. Blasted into bedrock, the shelter ran like a tunnel all across the town, was lighted and roomy, and had toilets and air fans. We saved spaces for our friends, munched on hardtack, and passed the time talking or playing word games. Often we slept. Some grown-ups didn't appreciate our having fun; they wanted to hear the bombs falling— a long whistling sound—and guessing where they hit each time.

The next morning we heard that four hundred enemy bombers had flown over Helsinki. They had done a lot of damage. Ambulances howled for hours, transporting victims to hospitals or morgues. Flames and wreckages were all over. From that night on, Juhani slept with his clothes on. Soon we all did the same. The schools closed their doors, and families were encouraged to leave the city and live with friends in the country. Sweden was accepting Finnish children. Trainloads of them were sent through the northern parts of the countries. Among these children were my cousins Reijo, Pirkko, and Marjatta to whom we said good-bye in the basement of the main post office. Hundreds of children stood like a herd of cattle, solemn or crying, their name tags attached with string around their necks. My parents didn't even want to hear about sending us away.

## February 24, 1944

We braved another bombing of Helsinki, six hundred Russian bombers this time, before Mother announced that we were going back to Massilanmäki. We had spent three months there four years earlier. Now it was 1944, and I was thirteen. It was again winter, and we had extremely cold temperatures for weeks at a time. The snow lay deep on the ground when we arrived at the Massinens. Pentti was eighteen months old, Anja was seven, and Juhani eleven. Life went on normally within the limitations of tight rationing and the war news.

As before, trains came from the war, continuously passing our stop, day and night. They brought back tired and wounded soldiers, as well as the dead in cars marked with fir tree saplings. Coming from the west, trains took fresh soldiers—younger and younger ones—and ammunition and other supplies to the front line.

This time Mother enrolled us in school, Juhani and Anja at an elementary school five kilometers away where they skied daily. I took an early morning, ice-cold train to Savonlinna, the city twenty-five kilometers away, where I attended an all girls' school, and returned home every evening.

I was behind in every subject, especially in math and German, which I had not had at all. I studied on the train and at the home of the son of Antti Massinen where I spent my long lunch hour every day. But I also had fun with the kids, especially Tuovi, the oldest son, who was my age, and Ville, a cousin of theirs. We were avid readers and fans of Edgar Rice Burrough's Tarzan series. The weekly excitement for me consisted of waiting for the Saturday evening train, which might bring Tuovi and Maila, his sister, to us for the weekend. There were disappointments when nobody came, and surprises when Tuovi came alone.

Once in a while, instead of my usual local train, I took a long distance train home—if it planned to stop at Massilanmäki. I was interested in talking with the returning soldiers. One day, as I came in from school and entered the tupa, I met Mother and Aunt Hanna standing side by side, looking most alarmed. Mother, holding up a letter in her hand, wanted to know "all about it." The women had opened and read the only piece of military mail I ever received, an innocent note from one of the soldiers.

Every time the southern sky had an orange glow at night, we knew Helsinki was being bombarded. Savonlinna, being an important relay station, also received its share of bombings. In the southeast, battle fires colored the sky. The war was getting bloodier and fiercer; we knew many of the soldiers who came back wounded—or dead. There was less food, for the government raised its demands for food items for the war effort, and each farmhouse felt the squeeze.

## April 1944

My world despite the war consisted mostly of school happenings, where in addition to struggling with the main subjects, I learned to run hurdles in the gym and to jump on a see-saw type contraption.

## May 25, 1944

For the end-of-the year ceremony at school, I appeared in an aquamarine silk dress with black spots. I felt good in it while standing in front of the whole school singing a song about the skylark.

By the end of the school year Helsinki was being bombed less often, since the Soviet Union was now fighting Germany. We, therefore, returned to Helsinki, leaving Massilanmäki the day my school ended.

## August 1944

Before the end of the summer, Dad took a trip to Massilanmäki to bring Juhani home, and to represent our family at the military funeral of Aulis Massinen, who died at the age of nineteen defending his country in the most violent battle of the Isthmus of Karelia, a major offensive by the Russians, at the same time that the Allied Forces landed in Normandy. He was the same young man on whom I had spied four years earlier as he and his friend secretly smoked kessu, the home-grown tobacco. On September 19, 1944, Finland signed a peace treaty in Moscow.

*Chapter 12*

# Good-Bye School

**December 1946**

Mother's gifts always came in soft packages and were practical and regular. Dad's gifts were fewer and came in hard packages; I seemed to remember them better. One Christmas it was a two-layer xylophone on which I played many melodies. On the snowless Christmas of 1946, I received a large diary from him. It was a Christmas to remember for the abundance of culinary delights available after eight years of food shortage. My new diary lists five pounds of ham, sixteen pounds of Danish apples, American chocolate, Ovomaltine from Norway, and raisin soup, in addition to the usual rutabaga casserole, peeled potatoes, and so on. The only thing missing was rice pudding to go with the raisin soup.

As customary, we brought in the Christmas tree on Christmas Eve morning. When Dad came home from work, he placed the tree in its stand, the star on the top, and the candleholders with white candles on the stronger branches, an exacting job. Juhani, Anja, Pentti, and I hung the strings of Scandinavian flags, the silver garlands, and tinsel while listening to the declaration of Christmas peace coming traditionally from the Turku Cathedral via radio. Soon the wonderful smell of ham drifted in from the oven, making us hungry.

In 1946 when I was almost sixteen, Juhani, fourteen, and Anja, ten, fun with Santa depended on Pentti, who was four and still a believer. For his sake we followed the old act of answering nicely to Santa's questions about our behavior during the year, singing a song to him, and pretending his mask looked natural. All this for getting our presents handed to us!

On Boxing Day, the 26th of December, my friend Hellä came over to play a new game, "Stock Exchange," with us. We lit the candles on the tree, and nibbled on gingerbread cookies as we played. While playing, it started to snow, and we got excited about going to ski soon.

During Christmas vacation we read all the books we received as gifts.

"Everybody is reading, except Pentti," says a note in my diary. The best enjoyment during winter vacations was to sleep late, and from my bed in the kitchen, I watched the wind blow clouds of dry snow off the roof tops and the electrical wires.

## January 1947

We welcomed the new year 1947 at home reading books. Mother and Dad had gone to the theater. Since there was no lead, we skipped the tradition of dumping a scoopful of melted lead into a bucket of snow or water, watching the lead harden into intricate shapes that, when held in front of a light, threw shadows on the wall. In past years when we had done this, the fun part was interpreting the shadows and forecasting everybody's future.

At school, Pulla, the headmistress herself, took us one night on a field trip to Ursa, the star tower. The dome rumbled as it rotated and opened up for us to gaze through a telescope at magnificent Saturn with its rings and moons. On the same trip we rode on our school's unupholstered sleds down the toboggan runs of the Ursa slope. What a moment of thrill and awe it was with millions of stars above us!

## February 1947

For our ski vacation in the winter of 1947, Hellä, Juhani, and I took a train to Uncle Arvi's house at Imatra, a few hours' trip to southeastern Finland. There we boarded a bus to Virmutjoki, a village twenty-nine kilometers away. As we got off the bus, the bus driver kindly pointed the way to Laamala School, where Hellä's aunt taught.

The weather was cold with a lot of snow on the ground as we tramped down the unplowed road. After a while we met a girl, and I asked her how far Laamala School was. She said this wasn't the road at all. "But you can continue on this road until you come to the mill. You'll pass a gray cottage and a drying barn. Go up the hill, and there's the road!"

She spoke in the Karelian dialect familiar to Juhani and me, but strange to Hellä. Uncle Arvi lived only ten kilometers from the Russian border and about 160 kilometers from Värtsilä.

We thanked her and continued walking according to her instructions, which we repeated to each other. We never found any gray cottage or barn, but we did find a road that had not been plowed for some time. We followed it uphill and downhill and came to a crossroads. There we met a man, whom we asked which road to take. He pointed to the wider one saying, "That's the one, they say."

After three kilometers we saw a farmhouse through a young pine forest and a horse pulling a sled and driver. We thought we were there. But when we talked with an old man who was chopping wood in the yard, he told us that the road didn't go to the school at all. Three kilometers back, the road had turned to the school!

Again luckily, there was an alternate way. "Take this path following the fence through that gate. Pass the house and keep turning to the left, and you'll see the school there!" he said smiling.

We couldn't help but laugh while thanking him. Eventually, we did find the correct road that led to our destination; it was three kilometers long and took us through drifting snow banks. As we arrived, a thought struck us simultaneously, "What if Hellä's aunt wasn't at home, but on vacation like us?"

She didn't know about our coming. We knocked and knocked on the door, but got no answer for a while. Discouraged and tired, we sat down on the steps, resting our legs, when we heard a creaking sound, as if footsteps were coming down toward us. We were welcomed by the teacher herself.

The Laamala School was just the kind of country school I had been dreaming of since sixth grade. I wanted to be a teacher in a school like that. A big, red wooden building, two stories high in a clearing in the middle of the forest and the snow, its classrooms had high ceilings, cylindrical fireplaces that matched the height of the rooms, tall windows facing the forest, and rows and rows of wooden desks. We visited some of the rooms, though they were icy cold, not being in use. We wrote on the blackboards, sat at the desks and especially enjoyed playing the harmonium and singing.

That night we could have heated the sauna, but since we didn't have plans for staying overnight, we didn't. Hellä's aunt served us delicious food and baked goodies; we really were hungry. At dusk she sent us to get milk from a neighbor not far from the school. Since no one had recently used the path by the edge of the woods to the neighbor's house, it was under snow. Taking turns being the leader and breaking the trail, the other two followed in the leader's steps.

The evening was calm and beautiful. A beam of light on the snow told us we were approaching the neighbor's house. We knocked on the door and entered the dimly lit tupa, greeting the man and his wife and introducing ourselves and the purpose of our visit. We were invited to sit down on the bench. The fire in the stove-oven gave off warmth and lighted up the ceiling; there was a wonderful feeling of peace.

We had no trouble in carrying on a conversation with the people, for we soon found out that the husband had done his military retraining in Värtsilä, and his wife had been twice to Helsinki. As she told about her trip to Helsinki, she spun yarn with admirable ease. I knew how hard it was to keep the wheel and the spinner and the "fluffs" going at the same time. Pretty soon she stopped spinning, put on a sweater, picked up a bucket and lantern and went to the barn to milk.

By the time we returned to the school, it was dark. The wind had picked up and sighed in the fir trees, a sign of thaw. We had some tea, said a prayer, and talked before going to bed. For the night Hellä and I shared a single bed, Juhani was sent downstairs into another room, and the teacher herself slept on the kitchen table! Hellä and I kept each other awake with ghost stories for a while, hushing one another's giggles.

We returned to Uncle Arvi's house, elated about our adventure and found his entire family eager to hear it. We enjoyed telling them about the long roads. For dessert that night, Hellä and I whipped up a large bowlful of "air pudding" made of lingonberries and cream-of-wheat, which we had learned to make in school. While we cooled it off in the snowdrift and beat it to make it fluffy, the setting sun colored the western sky burning red-orange. At the same time from the opposite direction rose a cold, silvery moon. The dusk with its grip of cold made us hurry inside with our pink and fluffy pudding.

## March-April 1947

During the in-between seasons when we couldn't ski or skate or play baseball (*pesäpallo*), we took long walks. During one of those walks in April, I mentioned to Janne, with whom I was walking, that my liver hurt and that I felt sick. She suggested that I might have "yellow jaundice," a liver disease. Her mother had had it, and her symptoms had been the same. Sure enough, when Mother took me to the doctor, he agreed with Janne's diagnosis and recommended bed rest and thin oatmeal for nourishment. I was very sick and had a high fever and hallucinations for days. But a week later Dr. Wasenius (the one who had cured me of an earache in Värtsilä), pronounced me much improved and assured me that I could eat anything, even my butter ration. I should not attend school yet, however. So, for three weeks I studied the faint patterns of our wallpaper—a nightmarish venture with high fever—of the sparkling white, long tunnel that started there, the end of which I never reached, luckily perhaps.

One day I felt so good I took a walk with Pirkko. After that I stood in line for an hour to buy cream-of-wheat for which I had a craving. While in line, I could feel my temperature rising. The chills ran up and down my spine, and I felt sick again. But, after three weeks I returned to school, thin as a blade of grass, fearful of flunking the year.

Two new situations awaited me at school: we were being taught short-hand by a male teacher whom we named Napoleon (the only man in the entire "nunnery"!) and the start of catechism classes for those of us who had not yet had first communion. The classes were given by Rev. Virk-kunen, a young Lutheran minister, who was able to communicate with us. He even made us cry at times. Spring was in the air with many expectations; our first communion was waiting, school was ending, perhaps forever for many of us.

## May 31, 1947

"Now that school was almost over and we were about to graduate" my diary said, "it was with sadness that I walked to it for the very last time on the 31st of May, 1947. With sadness I also saw the familiar basswood tree, under which we had so many times gathered, for the last time."

The school had a festive atmosphere that day—both happy and sad—as we, the graduating class, sat as guests of honor in front of the music room nervously waiting for our names to be called by the headmistress. We received our diplomas, then sang the touching hymn about the coming of the summer, the one sung at the end of each school year at every school in Finland: "Jo joutui armas aika ja suvi suloinen. Kauniisti joka paikkaa koristaa kukkanen . . ." (Summer has arrived, the dearest of seasons, and flowers cover the land . . .).

"Seitsikko": Laila, Bisse, Nita, Anja, and Inge.

Chapter 13

# "Seitsikko," the Group of Seven

**July 1947**

The summer of 1947 was hot for Finland but relieved by refreshing thundershowers. Helsinki hosted the World Championship Games and filled with curious country folk.

The exciting addition to our family was our first pet ever, a fox terrier puppy, Tomi, from my Aunt Greta in Järvenpää.

Dad had recently purchased a piece of land in Mankkaa, part of the compensation Finland's government gave to those Karelians who had lost their land to the Russians. We would build our very own home on it. My friends and I made several bicycle trips there, enjoying the eight-mile ride over seven challenging bridges, as well as the beauty of the ocean and the countryside.

**September 1947**

In the fall, instead of enrolling at the Preparatory School, Pirkko and I continued at the insurance company, where we had mutual friends with whom we socialized. At Mankkaa, Juhani and I planted ten apple trees, many berry bushes and flower bulbs—fifty-five plants altogether—on a stormy, rainy day. Our rubber boots had clods of clay six inches thick clinging to them, which made the planting very difficult. In the fall also we buried our puppy at Mankkaa, planting a rose bush over her. She had died of distemper, the sickness of sicknesses for pets. There are ten pages on grief in my book and a poem for "the little ray of sunshine."

Another disappointment for me was that "Hoosianna," the advent hymn wasn't sung at the service I attended. I was hoping for the usual lifting of the spirits, the effect it had on me.

## November 1947

The good news was the forming of Seitsikko, the group of six girlfriends and me at Vallininkuja 7. At Bisse's we celebrated "Little Christmas" with a small tree, small gifts and a tea, and talked business. For seven years we had been friends and had shared most everything with each other. Anja, my sister, was now eleven; Bisse was twelve; Inge, Magi and Laila fifteen, and Nita and I almost seventeen. We met weekly, had tea and pastries, received mail from each other—on secrets and feelings—discussed things, played games, danced, and did sports together.

I was sick with the flu over Christmas and reminisced over our lost puppy: "Through the flickering flame of a candle, as I looked at her picture . . ." Anja and I attended church on Christmas morning—tramped to Kallio Church through a major snow storm. After Christmas I received a card from Tuovi in Savonlinna, which made me very happy.

## December 31, 1947

On New Year's Eve at Laila and Nita's house, while the others were having fun, I wrote a melancholy poem called "In the Moonlight." I was sad because I had found blood in my sputum and was afraid I had tuberculosis. Finally I approached my father about it, and was comforted and encouraged, for he said the blood probably came from my throat; he had heard how hard I was coughing. I perked up and got well quickly.

Before Seitsikko started *Seitsikko News*, I wrote and illustrated a chronicle about the girls. It referred to Inge's endless grooming of her ash-blonde hair and looking out her window to see and be seen by Leo, who had recently said "hi" to her, after having ignored all of us for years. The lyrics refer to Magi as admirer of Jo in *Little Women*, and to the haunting spirits she kept seeing in her dreams. Laila's impatience with run-away stitches in her knitting is brought out, as are her bible studies. Bisse was always in a good mood, and "kept our ship on course." Nita, our honorary doctor by her own suggestion, was "given the floor" in the chronicle, because her presence was appreciated. She was often absent due to her work at the hospital. The part on Anja is short due to the fact that most of what I wrote on her is missing.

To show the extent of our craving for sweets after years of deprivation, here's what we had with our tea at one of our meetings: doughnuts, apple tarts, Alexander's tarts, and bebés.

## February 1948

Shrotide (Laskiainen) occurs in February when the snow conditions are suitable for every kind of outdoor fun. Because of the sun's warming of the snow during the day and subsequent freezing at night, the snow "carries" a person and a sleigh, sled, or cardboard. Seitsikko plus my brother Juhani made the most of the conditions on the slopes by the Eläintarha railroad tracks that year. Carrying a piece of cardboard each, we walked up the slopes and came down on our boards time after time, loving it. We discovered and tried out many slopes, and got so carried away with fun that it was past 11:00 PM when we returned home. On the table at home, Mother had our Shrovetide pullas (something like hot cross buns) waiting for the three of us.

## February 1948

I did a lot of skiing that year in company of different friends. With my school friends we braved the winds on the ice of the Gulf of Finland as we skied to one of the islands. With Thelma, also a school friend, I skied to the home of another friend under too warm ski conditions; the snow stuck to our skis badly, and we had to stop often to scrape them clean. The going was slow and exhausting and made us hungry by the time we reached our destination. Because of the hard times, all our friend could offer us to eat was carrots from her cellar. Luckily she also had a special cream for treating our skis, and our return trip to Helsinki was much easier. Half the fun of cross-country skiing was resting on top of the slopes—for talking. Another joy I remember came after skiing with Nita in the woods; we reached a clearing and saw the Evening Star's first twinkle in the darkening sky.

## April 1948

An excursion at Easter—without skis—took us to Mankkaa, our piece of land, where we build a fire in the yard (there was no cabin yet) and made tea, and later dried our socks by the fire. For nothing better to do, we jumped over ditches full of water, at times making it without falling in, other times not. It was fun especially for Inge and Laila, because they were getting much teasing, as well as attention and assistance from my brother, who was their age. The funniest part came after walking five kilometers to the nearest railway station. Juhani's shoes gave out; both soles came loose, making a interesting clippety-clap sound at the Helsinki station, where we were embarrassed by the attention we received.

## May 1948

It was the time of white and blue anemones that grew wild in the woods. They made up the traditional Mother's Day bouquet to go on the table. We made the coffee that morning, and sang Mother a special song.

Tiny buds formed on the apple trees and bushes we had planted on our land. Soon I would gather a bouquet of narcissus for Juhani's first communion; he would appreciate a bouquet of flowers he had planted himself.

Almost every day I walked to work, taking the pretty path that followed the bay and ended near the National Theater.

Just before Juhannus that year we got a new puppy, Terri, from a litter at my Aunt Greta's house; we helped shorten the tails of all of the little pups. Terri was vaccinated against distemper and stayed well. She loved to go for walks and ride the bus to Mankkaa, where she ran free, swam in the pond, and helped us by tearing hunks of turf into pieces. We were preparing the soil for growing potatoes and vegetables.

## June 1948

Lake Urja was one of several lakes about thirty kilometers west of Helsinki. Seitsikko had formed the plan of going camping and had purchased the necessary camping gear from the U.S. Army supply store. Among the items we bought was a tent without end pieces, which we sewed on using my mother's sewing machine, breaking many needles on the stiff canvas. In preparation of the expedition, Juhani helped us by mapping a route, and we found out which bus to take.

The importance of the bus route lay in the group of boys we met. Dubbed "The War Gang" because they had a lot of army gear and were kind of loud, they seemed to be experienced campers and frightened us about not having a permit for camping at Urja. When they checked the route marked on our map, they said theirs was easier and invited us to join them. We stuck to our plans, but were followed by two younger campers, who later taught us how to flip pancakes in the air. First we waited nearly six hours for a bus.

We chose a spot for our tent on the western bank of Urja, between two pine trees. The sky was high and very blue, and the lake shimmered in the sunshine. We gathered rocks and wood for the fireplace, ate our sandwiches and, in the evening, sat around the fire talking and singing while watching the flames dance.

Then we heard twigs breaking and voices nearby; the "gang" was on its way. What to do? What if they were rowdy? We decided to take it easy and allow them to come for a visit. They came with their pocket Gramophone and had plenty of music. Ossi, their leader, wore a military "boat hat." We soon found we could trust him, for all the boys obeyed him surprisingly well.

Only my sister Anja slept that night; the rest of us talked while waiting for the sun to rise. It didn't happen but started raining instead. At first the sound of raindrops on the tent sounded like music, but pretty soon the canvas got wet because the seven of us leaned against the walls—seven of us in a two-man tent.

Our departure from Helsinki had been difficult, what with the bus delay. Our departure from Urja was difficult because we had so much to carry, and everything was wet. The tent alone weighed a ton. We also got lost, and the last bus had left before we got to the bus stop. But we got in the back of a truck, and even if we froze, being wet, we were grateful.

Our excursion to Lake Urja was only the initiation to the tens of excursions we took during the next four years. We got to know Ossi's gang very well.


## July 1948

After four years I returned to Massilanmäki where twice our family had found refuge during the war and where I had had "matters of the heart" ever since. Now at seventeen I came by boat through the lovely Saimaa waterways to Savonlinna, the city where I attended the all-girls' school and learned German in 1944. The trip was idyllic, with white ships serenely passing each other on the smooth, dark waters of the chain of lakes. Gentle ripples, picturesque islands with bending birches and boat houses—there were also pretty sunsets—but also a lonely cabin.

Manu, the oldest son of the Massinens of Massilanmäki, the one who was in the Air Force during the war, met me at the harbor. In his thirties and balding, he was tall and fun. I had mentioned my red hat to him, and that was how he found me. After exchanging news, we walked to Tuovi's house where—my heart leaping and stopping—I again met Tuovi. He had grown and changed, growing taller than I and sturdier, but still had his warm smile. After an initial shyness, we found something to say to each other.

At the Massinen's household everything was as before, even the pitiful sauna still stood, now surrounded by a yellow sea of wheat. The best sound I had heard for a long time was that of the cowbells as Eero brought the cows in for milking. Aunt Hanna and Impi with her twin sons were there, and we enjoyed talking.

At Tuovi's house one day we had fun making a cake, which we beat by hand, Tuovi and I. For dinner that day the table was set only for four: Maila, Tuovi, his cousin Ville, and me. We had much fun with photo albums; Ville found amusing things wrong with the people in the pictures. We talked about movies and movie stars; the boys liked Rita Hayworth and Loretta Young best. We went to the movies, the boys in suits and with their hair combed back with water. We enjoyed ourselves so much that I almost missed my train to Massilanmäki late at night. The best part was when Tuovi and I ran all the way to the station through the streets and down the basswood lane.

During the week Tuovi came to see me, and we were quite comfortable with each other. We discussed many things, even the ticks on the cows, sometimes in English—which interested Manu especially. The most exciting happening was Impi's taking a photo of Tuovi and me under a blossoming apple tree. Encouraged by her, and directed by Manu's wife, Hilja, Tuovi put his arm around my shoulders, and I felt jubilant.

Back in Helsinki I wrote a poem called "For Amor" and thought of Tuovi's farewell smile and wink for a long time thereafter. At that point I concluded that the summer had been the best in my life so far. The pictures under the apple tree turned out fine.

### August 1948

Seitsikko spent many weekends at the cabin at Mankkaa, where we ran races and listened to the music on my father's Gramophone. Our newest record was "Mona Lisa" sung by Nat King Cole in his velvet-soft voice that we loved. On the other side was "An Irish Lullaby" sung by Bing Crosby. We played both sides until we had most of the words copied and learned.

Nita and I often took long walks on the bay road and discussed most intimate topics. We were reading *Every Man's Psychology,* and wondered about the things we learned from it. At seventeen the purpose of life for me was learning everything possible, and I was reading books of "high category" in order to "civilize myself."

Pirkko and I joined the Finnish-American Society where we learned English from a young woman from the United States. One memorable phrase we learned from her was, "Holy cow!" For a textbook we used *Reader's Digest* which was beyond us at the time; we had to look up every other word in the dictionary, which, in the evening hours, made us silly. We ran into many funny words while searching for something else.

### September 1948

We also joined a French class where the teacher was an older lady from Switzerland and spoke with us only in French. I quickly learned to pronounce and read French. But since Pirkko and I froze after each class, we quit going. The icy wind on Frederick Street, where the classes were held, cut all the way into our innards.

*Chapter 14*

# Orienteering

**November 1948**

In the fall of 1948 when I was still seventeen, the insurance companies in Helsinki held a contest in orienteering. Pirkko and I, being the youngest at Suomi Insurance Co., were chosen to represent it, supposedly to bring honor to the company. It fell to Kris Niemelä, a young married man, to coach us by teaching us to read topographic maps and use the compass. On four Sundays Pirkko and I practiced orienteering in unfamiliar locations, looking for check points and getting beneficial exercise by running through all kinds of terrain. We did quite well and were exhausted at the end of each day.

The closer the date of the contest came, the more nervous Pirkko and I became. The frosty Sunday morning of the contest saw us among other nervous contestants on the train to Savio.

Pirkko was the first to be sent off; my time came ten minutes later. I folded the green card in my left pocket. In my left hand I held a piece of cardboard; in my right pocket were a pencil and a small ruler. I blew my nose, and waited . . . five seconds more, the map was put in my hand, then: GO! I took two steps and fell flat on my stomach, having slipped on a tree root. The people behind me laughed, and I trembled wild with panic. I was panting and my eyes filled with water, but I would not give up. I took my position and knelt on my right knee, placed the now-broken cardboard and the map on my left knee, and using my ruler, drew the connecting lines between the check points. I took the direction with the compass, placed my pencil across it, blew my nose, wiped my eyes and started running through the crunchy, strange woods and bogs.

A half hour passed without my finding even the first check point. My head pounded, my brain telling me that the check point had to be to the left of me. Magically it was! After my green card was stamped by the attendant, I took a new direction, deciding to cross a bog to catch up on time lost. When I came to the edge of the frozen bog I slowed down, spread my arms and walked as lightly as I could not to break the ice. I thought I had made it when the ice around me suddenly cracked and popped wide open, plunging me into its icy waters up to my knees. I scrambled out and reached a hummock, safe.

The second and third check points were easier to find, and by the fourth one I had gained in skill. At the goal line, the hot juice handed to me was most welcome, for I felt raw inside my throat and lungs. I found my name on line seven of the scoreboard, with the time 1:42:24 next to it, and felt great! Pirkko came in a little later. We got much praise from all levels at the company, and, as a prize, the company gave us a day off. I had placed seventeenth out of the seventy-four contestants!

## December 28, 1948

On the day of the Innocents, the 28th of December, we celebrated Dad's fiftieth birthday with an open house. Flower arrangements kept coming throughout the festive day. One of the older girls in our complex took a family picture. In it Tuula, my sister-to-be, appeared only as a contour of Mother's stomach.

## March 1949

In the new year 1949 the only remaining shortage was money. Oranges and shoes were available without coupons. About the only thing coupons still were needed for was cotton fabric. The times were clearly better, and "there shouldn't be anything obscuring one's happiness," says my diary. But we had major problems with our living arrangements, for we had grown in size and in numbers, too. Our mother was expecting a baby in April! Everyone's rights were being violated; we too often raised our voices and accused each other and grew progressively more irritated.

Juhani spoke up, letting Dad "have it." He pointed out how foolish it was to bring another person into a living space already suffocating. With tears in his eyes Dad said, "Son, when the time comes, make sure you do things right in your family!"

There was hope for us, though, for Dad had started our house at Mankkaa. He had dug the foundation by hand, removing tons of heavy clay to three meters deep, while standing in water. This was done in addition to his regular work at the shipyard. We had a government loan, but more funds were needed for building materials.

When, with my earnings, I purchased a brand-new bike and a fashionable spring coat, Mother remarked that other needs existed besides new clothes, and that I had been selfish. I owed Aunt Linda for part of the bike's cost. I guessed there would be no vacation that summer.

## April 14, 1949

On a sunny, crisp day in the middle of April, Tuula was born, big and perfect and clearly resembling Dad. Summer was coming, and we loved the baby, who seemed to understand that she had to grow up fast. At the age of five months she stood up in her carriage. Her constant companion was our dog, Terri, who had decided that Tuula was *her* baby. When we noticed the dog's swollen breasts, I called the veterinarian. He informed me that our dog was experiencing a pseudo pregnancy, and that cold compresses would relieve the condition.

At Mankkaa we were busily planting potatoes. When more seed potatoes were needed one day, Pirkko, Bisse and I, riding our new bikes, went to get some in town. Some of our apple trees were already blooming.

## June 1949

Suddenly Mamma, my mother's mother, died at the age of sixty during a goiter operation, one that many of the women in Mother's family had had. We were shocked and saddened by her unexpected departure. The grave-side services, the grief and the tears have blended to a blur with other similar services. We still pay visits with flowers to her throughout the year and light a candle for her on Christmas Eve.

## July 1949

I did go on a trip after all that summer—this time with Pirkko to her grandmother's place in Häme, in the center of Finland. For a few relaxing days we rowed to different islands where we picked berries and made coffee on an open fire. Lake Päijänne is known for its fjord-like sides, cliffs and deep waters. Häme is famous for its rich yogurt; we enjoyed eating it daily. Pirkko and I also spent time at the loom, clunking away while weaving a rug, the two of us together.

Perhaps the most tempestuous time in my life came during the years 1949 and 1950. Four young men entered my life through the many excursions we took to the lakes. They were: Ossi, Unski, Bror, and Osku.

Looking back now after forty years, Ossi was the puzzle, both irritating and interesting. A born leader, he controlled every move anyone in his team made, during camping trips or at other times. Since he had a telephone at his home—rare in those days—everyone reported to him. He decided situations and suggested moves, manipulating us all like a Greek god, arranging and mixing situations and people at will.

Since I could be reached by phone at work, most communications came through me, except when he was first seeing Inge and later Laila, who communicated directly with him. Anything concerning a camping trip was discussed between him and me and relayed to our teams. The trouble began when Ossi started deciding on my social interests, jealous of anyone showing an interest in me.

Ossi wasn't big or strong or dazzling by any means, but talking with him was fun. Over his brown hair he generally wore a military "boat" hat, his trademark. When he learned that we had an aquarium, he invited me on a trip to a pond that had cyclopes for it. Twice we took the bicycle trip, and twice I enjoyed catching pond life and eating apples in his orchard. There was no romance between us exactly, other than the situation itself: cool, clear nights, a stop at the Kiosk, and a cup of tea at our cabin. By insisting that I take his sweater to shield me from the cool night air—as I would have to pedal back to Helsinki alone—he showed gallantry, but at the same time he secured another encounter.

Unski was good-looking with blue eyes and wavy blonde hair, prominent lips and pensive wrinkles at the brow. He was also a stylish dresser and younger than I. We met on one of the trips to the lakes, and sat together in a hollow of a cliff by the water, talking. He owned at least sixty Gramophone records, which were played constantly on our camp-outs. We met at different places in Helsinki, but most of the time he was out of town or studying for exams. He carried my Seitsikko pin for good luck, he said. It had helped him in his Swedish and German exams and had won him the first place in an orienteering contest.

But the ghost of Tuovi hung over our relationship. Then one day he called to warn me about "some wild guys" who were going on the next excursion; he himself wasn't.

## August 22, 1949

The excursion was the best of all, for the company we had was really interesting, and Ossi again controlled his troops well. Ossi introduced my six girlfriends and me to the new boys, and that's how I met Bror. After dinner and the usual sitting and chatting around the campfire, Bror approached me from behind by touching my shoulder. We worked together on lodging for thirteen people. One tent became a storeroom. Somehow we were the last to retire for the night and found lots of things to talk about.

The next day, which was sunny and warm, Nita, Osku, Bror and I went rowing, the boys taking turns at the oars, rowing us around—at times in the true sense of the word. There was much splashing, crooked rowing and water in the boat. The paddles also got away many times. Just as we had straightened out and were doing well, the momentum was disrupted by either Bror or Osku grabbing hold of some water lily stems; that stopped the going. The boys picked water lilies for Nita and me, and together we made sun shades out of the leaves. The day was perfect, there was no hurry, and the company was delightful.

Bror took me to the movies one night, and Inge and Reijo, his friend, went dancing with us on an outdoor platform. The night was beautiful, and Glenn Miller's music wonderful for dancing.

## September 1949

On September 2, my name's day, Bror and Reijo joined us at our cabin at Mankkaa. He brought me a bouquet of blue violas and danced only with me. Some of the other boys showed up also, but Ossi only stopped by to hand me his bouquet of flowers. There was a feeling about Bror and me that made the girls smile at us in a special way. We had a romantic walk in the night with the glowworms on the banks of the unpaved road. Later that night the boys rode away on their bikes, and so did Bisse and I early in the morning—to Helsinki through a very thick fog.

Bror and Reijo invited Inge and me to their party at Bror's home one Saturday night. He lived with his father and an older brother, Göran, outside the city. Somehow the men had produced a great banquet of things to eat and to drink. We did a round of cheers and danced tenderly to such favorites as "Tango Bolero" and "I'd like to get you on a slow boat to China. . . ."

The trouble began when Göran began cutting in on our dance. He was having disagreements with his girl, and he kept pulling Bror away to talk to him. He asked me weird, disturbing questions. I was puzzled, and Bror quiet. The evening lost its magic because of Göran.

We ran into Unski at the railway station, on our way home in the morning. ("Well, good morning to you!" he said to the four of us sarcastically.) We knew Ossi would get the news fast. In the next few days I received many phone calls, but not one from Bror. My feelings were hurt, because I was in love for the first time, I knew then. Yet, I had a hunch everything was lost.

Trying to find out about Bror, I met with Göran. When Bror finally called and asked me out, I said no, hoping he would call again. But he never did, and our beautiful romance died there, leaving at least me brokenhearted.

## October 1949

My friend Hellä, who had been hospitalized since spring, was slowly dying of tuberculosis. The medicines that had cured her brother did nothing for her. It was sad to visit her toward the end, for there was little to say or do. The fruits or candy Pirkko and I took went directly into her cabinet. Her appetite was gone, her breathing laborious, and the coughing attacks took every bit of her strength. She lay almost sitting up, thin and pale. Her fever chart at the foot of the bed showed constant high peaks, and more and more frequently we found her bed empty and her in an isolation room.

Earlier when Hellä still could talk and laugh with us, she wanted to hear all about what everybody was doing. She told us jokes she had learned from her fellow patients. According to one of them, they all were members of the "Feet First Club," she said pointing to the morgue.

When the chief surgeon of our Insurance Company heard about the many visits Pirkko and I had paid to the sanitarium, he sent for us, and after finding us healthy, vaccinated us with Calmet vaccine to rebuild our resistance to tuberculosis.

## November 1949

In November my skin problems flared up so badly that I ended up in the Dermatology Hospital for fourteen days. I was down in spirits, gray as the November sky. There were no stars. I was examined by a group of doctors and doctoral candidates; they asked questions, took notes, drew on my skin under different lights. They prescribed antihistamines that made me sleep all the time, and finally decided to put me through the coal-tar treatment.

My arms and legs were painted with the vile stuff and wrapped up like a mummy for twenty-four hours at a time. Every morning the patients met in the dressing room (pun intended!) where the dressings were removed. The ointment on me was wiped off like paint with remover, and my skin was then examined by the professor himself. During the fourteen-day stay I grew a completely new skin.

My friends from home and from work paid me visits often. After I called Ossi, he became the most frequent visitor. He brought books to read—series and thick volumes—and we talked while walking the corridor or sitting on a bench. Unski visited my house twice while I was away, but never showed up at the hospital. From Bror I heard nothing.

Knitting a three-color sweater for my brother Juhani kept me busy when I wasn't asleep or reading. I was released from the hospital on Little Christmas, which we celebrated at Laila and Nita's in the company of Ossi's gang.

## December 24, 1949

As I was walking to see Hellä at the sanitarium on Christmas Eve morning, I thought the weather being nice and crisp might help her to breathe more easily. While waiting for the visit I talked with a patient in the hallway. When she knew that I had come to see Hellä, she broke into sobs, and told me that she had died that morning in her mother's arms. She was buried on New Year's Eve at the age of nineteen. Many of her school friends attended the reception following the internment.

## January 1950

One day Ossi appeared at the door at work, waiting for me. He repeated this on four consecutive days for reasons that remained a mystery. We talked as we walked along Alexander Street, window shopping at Stockman's and stopping for a cup of hot chocolate. Once we went to a non-stop movie—a novelty for me. The only seats available—after we found them in the dark—were in the last row, and I had trouble seeing what was on the screen; my glasses remained in my purse. He called again in February just to say hi.

My nineteenth birthday came and went leaving me with a leg in a splint, a skiing injury lasting three weeks. My girlfriends and I visited "our breathing hole," the cabin at Mankkaa, often. Once Pirkko and I took four hours to ski there with Terri, our dog. We also skied in the Folk Skiing Contest between all of the Scandinavian countries; Finland won.

## February 1950

During the ski vacation Seitsikko spent four days again at the cabin— our escape from the families. The ice flowers on the window did not thaw out, but shone in rainbow colors when light bounced on them. (By Easter there was so much snow, the cabin seemed to be sitting in a hole.) The path we dug to it was narrow—the width of a shovel—and so deep we couldn't see the tops of our heads over the snow piles.

During the vacation, I skied down the most challenging slope—almost like a ski jump—without falling down. The slope was so steep, my skis stuck out in the air at the start, and at the landing area where the speed and wind engulfed me, I struggled with a washboard-like terrain.

When Inge and I went skating one night, we ran into Osku and his friends, whom we did not know. The boys had been playing ice hockey and had their sticks with them. Osku, one of Ossi's group, had been on every summertime excursion we had had, and was the quietest of all the boys. He watched everything from the sidelines. Now among his friends, however, he was the spokesman, and he totally surprised Inge and me by taking the lead. We formed a long chain with the boys and skated to music coming from the loudspeakers. We requested pieces of music familiar to us, such as "Buttons and Bows," "Riders in the Sky," and "The Three Caballeros." Osku paid for the first round of hot juice at the concession stand. We stood around the fire, warming up and talking. On the rink we fell down more than once in a big pile of people, hockey sticks and skates.

We went skating three times. Then one day I got a call from Ossi making a date for Osku with me! He had been informed again! We saw four premier movies together—mostly Abbott and Costello films. There was nothing but friendship between Osku and me.

# June 1950

In the beginning of summer my family left for Mankkaa for the entire summer; only Juhani and I stayed in town, working. Juhani's exciting new interest that summer was cycling. He competed in street competitions and at the Velodrome on a bike so light I could lift it up with one finger. Since the contests were rough, after each one, I acted as his private nurse, patching him up.

In June Seitsikko and Ossi's gang went to one of the lakes again, and in July Pirkko and I took our first trip abroad, a guided bus tour to Lapland, northern Sweden and Norway. We picked sea shells from the Arctic Ocean, climbed icy mountains, danced under the midnight sun, and slept under down-filled comforters in Tromsö. I loved every minute of it, and my longing for travel got its start; the travel bug had bitten me.

At Mankkaa: Bee #1—neighbors, family, friends, and our fox terrier, 1952.

*Chapter 15*

# International Voluntary Workcamp Ruukinsalo

**April 1951**

A change in direction in my life took place in the spring of 1951, when Pirkko and I had been out of school and working for the Suomi Insurance Company for four years. Retirement benefits did not concern us, and we couldn't even think of staying at our jobs for much longer. We really did not know what to do.

One day we took a walk during our lunch hour, stopping at the corner of the modern-day Forum, then a huge hole surrounded by a board fence. Among the announcements on the fence was one about an international voluntary workcamp, inviting Finnish youth to participate in helping new farmers in northern Finland clear land. Young people from different countries did the work. (The United States Congress created the Peace Corps in 1961 for a similar purpose.) Working with people that spoke different languages provided an opportunity for Pirkko and me to use our hard-learned languages—mainly German and English.

Pirkko and I looked at each other and decided to find out more. KVT, the initials for the Finnish camp organization, supplied us with details, and we signed up. That very evening we eagerly started making lists of useful words in both English and German. We studied the brochures of the organizers of these international camps: The American Friends Service Committee, or the Quakers. Their goal was to help post-war Europe by organizing international, voluntary workcamps in places needing help. Scholarships were available for foreigners. By working side by side with villagers the young people of several countries shared a common goal that created understanding and good will among different nationalities. (For example, the Germans burned Lapland as they retreated in 1944; we in turn had many German youths helping clear land in Lapland.)

**Summer 1951**

Although I didn't know it then, Seitsikko's excursion to Lake Urja that summer would be the last. In the evening of the Midsummer Day I returned from the excursion tired, dirty and quite content. I had less than thirty minutes to get washed and changed, a sandwich made, and my things packed into Juhani's knapsack. With the help of my friends Magi and Inge I made it, and caught the train to the north; Pirkko was there waiting for me.

From Kuopio we took a bus to Hankamäki School at Säyneinen, where we found ourselves among campers having supper at the long table. Soon we left for the camp at Ruukinsalo, pushing our belongings on the bikes for most of the eight kilometers, for the road was soft and muddy. Pirkko was one of the campers at the school we had just left.

The day being beautiful and the company interesting, I didn't feel the distance at all. There were only four Finnish campers there: Kalevi, Lasse, Pessi, and I. Girls had quarters at the attic of the Oinonen's house, and the boys had theirs at a neighbor's. At five-thirty Mrs. Oinonen knocked on our floor with a broom from below to wake us for making breakfast. All morning we unpacked and accommodated dishes and supplies and, in the afternoon, left to do marketing and receive new campers at the bus stop.

We received Kay Reese from England and Rose Perry and Martin Forrester from the United States. From the moment I shook hands and welcomed them to Finland, I knew I would like our camp. We started speaking English the best we could—and in bed that night I thought of having spoken English for five kilometers for a start.

I saw Martin first, through a cloud of smoke from his Finnish pipe. When he removed it from his mouth, a set of pearl-white teeth flashed as he said, "Hello!" The villagers soon gave him the name "Pippuri" or "Pepper," because he was black.

Rose was to become a friend for life. Her Boston English was a bit unclear to us at first; in fact we understood Kay's British English better because that's what we had learned in school. Rose was slender with shoulder-length dark hair and special dark-blue eyes, and her voice was a little raspy. I admired her musical ability in harmonizing any song instantly. At home she played the French horn in an orchestra.

Kay had short brown hair, was stout, easy-going and witty. Her contribution to our song collection was a round: "Bluebells are bluebells, bluebells are blue, bluebells are, bluebells are, bluebells are blue."

Kalevi, our leader, was twenty-seven, tall and slender with dark-blonde hair and a receding hairline. He was an elementary school teacher from near Helsinki.

Lasse, about Kalevi's age, short and stocky, was quiet and spoke softly, and had a good sense of humor, like Kay.

Pessi was the head teacher of a kindergarten in Turku. Tall and slen-

First Workcamp, 1951: Kay, Pessi, Pippuri, Sinikka and Kalevi.

der, with long dark hair combed back, she was also very gentle and motherly.

All four Finns were speaking English for the first time, and we kept
correcting each other, having studied the language for many years.

Our job was to clear land for farming by removing tree stumps from
the fields, to cut down trees in sections of forest, to make hay, and to help
at the sawmill. The Oinonen family at whose house we lived consisted of
Mr. and Mrs. Oinonen and their two young sons. Mr. Oinonen had fought
in the war against the Russians, and had been granted his "cold farm" as
reward for his efforts.

As soon as we got our household in order and filled the mattress bags
with straw, we were ready for work. On the first day, Rose, Kay, Kalevi
and I sawed down skinny trees while Pippuri and Lasse played carpenter
and made a table and benches for us. One day Pippuri disappeared for an
hour and a half to get a drink of water. When he finally returned, he carried a pail of fresh water with a ladle bouncing on it, and a trayful of crackers with apple butter on them for us. We smilingly accepted both and
instantly forgave him.

One evening after ten o'clock when Pippuri decided to have a sauna
with two other men, we expected him to return promptly and left Lasse by
the sauna, just in case. Pippuri, however, lasted as long as the other men
and took more steam than they did. The other men came out pinker, and
Pippuri blacker than before. He was blowing hot air and wiping his head
with a towel as he sat down on a bench in the tupa. He said that in spite of
having almost died in the sauna, he loved it! All of the foreigners eventually
learned at least to tolerate the steam and loved the magnificent internal-
external cleansing effect.

To discuss our work plans and schedules, we held our first community meeting at the Oinonen's tupa one evening. It filled up mostly with men, and it took a while for them to feel comfortable with us. Pippuri saved the day by performing a song about Miss Mousey's wedding, the refrain of which says, "Boom, boom." It became his hit song from then on. That got everybody participating in the "boom, boom," and clapping joyously at the end. Pippuri did several encores, yet left us wanting more. He was our main attraction and greatest contribution to the village!

One day as we pulled stumps for a family by the river, Kalevi was teaching Finnish to Rose. One of the phrases she learned was *"ehkä niin,"* meaning "maybe so." While the two were doing dishes later that evening, Rose used the phrase twice successfully and completely surprised Kalevi when she answered *"todellako?"* meaning "really?" to his suggestion about *"Suutele minua,"* meaning "Kiss me!"

One evening in the attic the girls enjoyed listening to the rain on the slanted roof. Kay and Rose were writing letters home. I could hear Pippuri singing downstairs, and someone played a recorder. In my letter home I mentioned that I was the only one who heard Mrs. Oinonen's knocking at five-thirty each morning. It was my job to wake up everyone—in English, to be sure. In my letter I also said that Pippuri lay down to rest at least as often as brother Juhani did at home.

Kitchen duty included marketing, preparing three meals a day, doing dishes and scrubbing the floor, but it was fun in the company of others. And more had arrived! Kikka, a language teacher, Reimund from Germany, Aino, Maiki, Ken from England, Jim from the United States of America, and Siru, our nurse, plus the four original ones. The foreigners pronounced Pessi's name as "Pässi," meaning "ram," and mine "Seneca" or "Senecker" in British English. We spent another cozy evening in the attic with the rain drumming on the roof. Pessi brought up a cake she had baked, and Ken prepared English tea for us. We studied English and Finnish, Kalevi played his violin, and Pippuri taught me a song. Soon we all joined in singing.

The last three days of my three-week stay at the camp were spent with Pippuri at the sawmill. Since I was the only female among many men, I was the object of their teasing; how weak women were for men's work, among other things. Therefore, I did not complain or let them know that my back was about to break or my arms hurt badly after lifting, carrying and placing only a few sawed boards in the stack. I loved the smell of sawdust, got used to the work and proved the men wrong.

During coffee breaks I served as an interpreter as we discussed many matters, including the American Negroes. Pippuri, with a faraway look in his eyes, answered the men. Then one day he discovered that he was in Finland representing his entire race, and didn't like the responsibility. He didn't want me to interpret that to the men. What a language situation I was in!

On our way back to the camp each day, we would swing our empty lunch bag between us as we walked down the road singing. Faces appeared at the windows of farmhouses we passed. When we entered the tupa, the rest of the campers were having dinner, but made room for us on the benches. They said they could hear us coming and laughed at my sunburned nose and at the stickiness of our sap-stained pants; the resin from the boards stuck us to the bench when we tried to get up.

The only scheduled activity other than work itself was daily Silent Meeting. We sat on the floor in a circle to meditate, concentrating on constructive and uplifting thoughts.

At Ruukinsalo workcamp I learned many international songs I still enjoy: "L'Amitie," "Dona Nobis," "The Ash Grove," "A la Claire Fontaine," "Haida, haida . . ." and "Waltzing Matilda." We sang all the time, it seems: on the fields while struggling with crowbars and stumps, in the woods sawing trees and fighting mosquitos, while traveling or resting.

Back in Helsinki it had been raining for days, and people were losing their hard-earned tans; they were not very cheerful at the insurance company where I worked. In August Pirkko and I went back to Hankamäki where the post conference was held, and in a huge circle holding on to each others shoulders, sang the lovely parting song "L'Amitie."

"The Laplanders," Rose, Kay and Reimund, who had hitchhiked to Lapland, surprised me one day by calling me at work. We met, had dinner at my home and went to see a Russian movie. Soon Kay left for London, and Rose and Reimund for Berlin. From there Rose continued to Paris, and eventually to Boston. How painful those farewells were!

*Chapter 16*

# Camp Autiosaari, 1952

Finland hosted the Summer Olympics in 1952, and Helsinki filled up with people from all over the world. Colorfully dressed people speaking many different languages walked the streets and crowded the stores and the cafes. Exotic flags streamed in the wind atop tall, white flag poles. Music and traffic noise and excitement—Helsinki was ready for the big event, for which it had been preparing since the end of the war.

I had purchased two tickets for the most important event in track and field, and took Pentti, who was almost ten. Before entering the gate, we purchased two ice-cream cones to take along, but just as Pentti was about to lick his ice cream, it fell to the ground. We could hardly believe our eyes! But Pentti was given another scoop free, and we recovered from our disappointment nicely.

My summer vacation was to be spent at Camp Autiosaari, situated at Kemijärvi, above the Arctic Circle, and reached by bus from Rovaniemi. Pirkko and I would again be clearing land and brushing up on our language skills in an international group of people. The scenery was peaceful, typically northern with its wind-shaped trees. It was nice and warm, though. My diary has only one page on the camp; not because it wasn't a good camp, or that the people were uninteresting, but because I kept many things inside, without trusting even my diary.

Four of us returned from the previous summer's camp: Kikka and Reimund, who were an "item," and Pirkko and I. This year we had a few Americans, a girl from New Zealand, two young men from Germany in addition to Reimund, and many Finns. Our job again consisted of cleaning land for planting grains. Mountains of pulled-out stumps stood on the fields after each day's work. At this camp I learned to speak German fairly fluently, for Horst, my constant partner, did not speak anything but German. My book says, "*Die schone Zeit*," or "The beautiful time" of my time in the camp. I was relaxed and dared to speak. I knew how to work and to organize. And I had admirers who, at times, fought over me! But we had nobody like Pippuri to entertain the villagers, however, but had to come up with something. We served coffee and crackers in the evenings, sang and held discussions, and went dancing on Saturday evenings with the local people.

Horst, who must have been about twenty-seven, had fought in the war. When asked, he would tell about being a prisoner of war. He had sharp, metallic-blue eyes, dimples and blond, sun-bleached hair cut to one length. He danced magnificently and sang well . . . privately. "Did you hear a street boy sing during the most wonderful night, when darkness wrapped itself around the wanderer?" I asked him to sing this to me many times. I learned a lot of German from him, and other things, too. When he told me that he was "ein Casanova," our situation just got more romantic, although at the same time I knew my limits, as well as those of any reasonable Finnish girl! Never had I had more idyllic summer evenings!

One morning just as we were getting ready to spread our members over several projects, we got the word that a mother of a young baby and a two-year-old boy had been taken to the hospital during the night, and that the family needed someone to substitute for her. Everyone looked toward me, for I had sisters and brothers. I volunteered. Horst took me to the place on his bike, and came for me late at night. What a day! Suddenly I had to know how to cook, feed, and take care of two young children—the baby was one week old—wash dishes and diapers. The children's father worked on the field, clearing land like everybody else. I was so busy that

**In Lapland 1952: Sinikka, Charles, Pirkko and Horst.**

the day went by fast. For some reason I didn't have to go back the next day. I was so glad!

At the camp we celebrated Finland's Armi Kuusela's becoming Miss Universe that year!

One frightening experience I had was an attempt at bare-back riding. I have no idea why I risked it. I was no horse rider. All I remember was that I was on a horse that took off and paid no attention to me clinging to its mane and ducking tree branches in the woods. I was stiff with fear. I stayed on until we returned to the start where all the people were. That's when I fell under the horse and saw the kinds of stars cartoons show when someone gets hit on the head. I was afraid the horse would step on me, too, but it didn't. I recovered and didn't complain about anything!

The camp ended at Rovaniemi where the post conference was held and all the campers gathered. All I remember of it was a song a German boy sang: "In the Mediterranean Sea sardines swim, aboo, aboo, aboo, aboo!" And we all joined in the "aboos" joyously. We said our painful good-byes and rode the train south, our thoughts far away. Then back to work.

## Fall 1952

In the fall a note in my diary says: "I'm alone at home in Helsinki; the rest of the family has been living at Mankkaa for six months now. Pretty soon the last of the furniture will be moved there. Good-bye, Vallininkuja, and the time of my youth; it's almost over! I'm going to my English class now, and after that to my choir party."

That autumn, for countless weekends, Christian, a Berliner whom I got to know at the camp in 1951 and who stayed to work in Finland, had been helping us at Mankkaa. He and I had the project of staining eighteen doors the color of mahogany, plus sanding and polishing them many times each. We also painted many window frames and attached windows to frames with putty. That kept us busy—no need for weekend plannings. We worked and talked and were content. Christian was speaking quite a bit of Finnish—enough to communicate even with my father. He talked a lot and laughed aloud a lot.

KVT's (The Workcamp Organization) Christmas Bazaar made history; among the many items received from campers around the globe to sell at our bazaar was a sackful of popcorn from America! The bazaar, held at the Old Student Building in the middle of Helsinki, attracted a steady flow of curious customers, especially since the smell of popping popcorn floated through the building, down the stairs and out onto Alexander Street! It must have been the premier, the introduction of popcorn to the entire country. It was very successful at that!

Our first Christmas at Mankkaa was white, with gusting wind and snow flurries. My brother Juhani came home for the holiday from his artillery unit. I was so glad he came. I had been wishing for his return. On Christmas Day I wrote in my diary, "The clock is ticking, the fish are treading water, and the candles on the tree are glowing sweetly. It's so peaceful!"

Just before Christmas we had an emergency in the middle of the night: Mother had terrible pains and had to be taken to a hospital (Kirurgi) in Helsinki. The doctors found out that she suffered from an allergic reaction to penicillin that she had been given by injection for her inflamed vericose veins. Her liver was bleeding!

The night was starless and stormy as we traveled in our neighbor's small car. On Lauttasaari drawbridge the car was tossed from side to side by the wind. We held our breaths and our seats. Mother recovered soon enough for Christmas and received a green sweater from Anja and me. We had been feverishly knitting it in the closet away from Mother's curious eyes.

After the holidays Anja and I tramped in the snow—up to our knees at times—to the Elanto store, a few kilometers away, to get our mail. The tramping was well worth our effort, however, for among the mail was a beautiful card from Horst. It had the Madonna and Child sketched in black ink.

The next entry in my diary took place five months later: "Since the last time, I have had my 22nd birthday (sigh), and I have made great plans for summer. I have received wonderful pictures from our camp last summer—from Horst via Christoffer—and suffered, as usual, from longing for someone. I'm tough at least!"

"Many of us from KVT spent the first of May at Kalevi's, and enjoyed it again. It was warm like in July, and we walked on the fields and played games. At Easter we all went to Pirttimäki with KVT. I was content. My skin has been better!" says my book, and continues:

"Juhani has been in the Army for almost six months now. He'll be going to Kokkola soon, for the shooting camp. Seija, his girlfriend, visited us after a long pause. She is pretty, blonde, and delicate. I don't think they are engaged yet. Anja took care of "her Arvo" at Vappu, and was telling us scary stories! Pentti, who is ten, will sing "The Land of Caanan" tomorrow in a combined boys' chorus at Grasa Church. He has a nice and powerful voice! He and I sing duets sometimes; he singing the soprano part, and I the alto. Tuula, who is four, learned to pronounce the Finnish "r" recently—her own way."

All through the wintry weekends Dad busily built our home, Mother taking care of the bills and the upkeep, at which she was very good. One of the "requirements" that made us smile was that her presence was "required" all the time. Otherwise Dad couldn't get inspired! Summer was approaching, and we had started to work the land. I was waiting for summer and hoping my plans for it would come true.

*Chapter 17*

# Workcamping in Germany

## June 1953

For five years I had been corresponding with Anne van der Ploeg in The Hague, Holland. This summer I would at last meet her on my way to southern Germany, where I would participate in another international, voluntary workcamp. All spring I had been planning and dreaming of my trip abroad; finally departure day arrived!

## August 8, 1953

One August morning I took the boat to Stockholm, then a train to Copenhagen, where I arrived early Sunday morning. I would have to wait six hours for the train to Holland. What could I do? I started walking in a nearby park, enjoying the coolness of the morning. After a while I sat down to check my schedule. A middle-aged lady sat down next to me, holding the leash of her dog.

I answered "Gud dag" to her greeting, the only Danish phrase I understood for the next six hours. I petted the dog's head while Mrs. Andersen talked in her throaty language, and I kept smiling and shaking my head in desperation. Whatever I said to her in Swedish, she understood; she was happy to know I came from Finland. She took me to her home, where she introduced me to her sculptor husband and found a young neighbor who spoke English and stayed to interpret.

The Andersen home was old-fashioned and interesting. Mr. Andersen's studio was a large, well-lighted room full of sculptures at different stages of completion. Some were covered, others not. For an appetizer we were given pieces of roasted pig skin—off the roast on the dining table.

With our interpreter we planned the afternoon activities: a guided tour of the King's Palace, then to Tivoli Gardens. The palace was one of the majestic government buildings of red brick with a turquoise-colored, oxidized roof. At Tivoli we sat under a colorful parasol watching the Ferris wheels, merry-go-rounds, and boats, while the music played. All I needed to do was smile and eat cake; I felt like a princess! But I didn't forget my train and made sure I got to the station on time. I hugged Mrs. Andersen and thanked her for the hundredth time, and from the train waved my hand saying in Swedish, "*Adjö, tack så mycket!*"

In those days one showed a passport entering and leaving a country, which interfered with sleep if traveling at night. As I left Denmark I showed my passport and had it stamped, only to have to do the same thing two minutes later for the German authorities. Only a few hours later as I was leaving Germany, I showed my passport again, and repeated the performance to the Dutch authorities.

I called Anne's home, where her mother answered and gave me instructions as to which tram to take to get to Sneeuwbalstreet 125, an address I wrote a hundred times in five years of correspondence. I found the van der Ploeg house without any difficulty; it was one pretty house among many pretty houses. Soon I heard footsteps and met Anne's mother, her dark hair high in front and the rest pulled back. She was warm and friendly, fairly tall, as was her husband, a gray-haired gentleman with cheerful brown eyes and a black beret on his head. He was the headmaster of a high school. Both welcomed me heartily and showed me Anne's room. We sat talking while waiting for Anne to return from work.

Anne found me in her room resting on one of the beds. We greeted one another shyly at first, but soon found plenty to talk about. She and I could have been sisters, for our height, weight, hair and eye color were the same! We walked the streets arm-in-arm shopping in Amsterdam, visiting Delft, famous for its white and blue porcelain. We went to see the polders and dikes that keep the sea away, except a year earlier when a dam broke and the sea surged in, damaging the land with its saltiness. It was very exciting to receive a bouquet of fresh flowers on each of the four mornings I stayed with the van der Ploegs; Anne's father himself presented them to me.

When it was time to go, the family van der Ploeg took me to the train which required only one hour to go through the entire country of Holland. Then we entered Belgium, and very soon I was again in Germany. By then I had shown my passport four times. The route through historic Cologne south to Wiesbaden was the beautiful Lorelei way, following the enchanting River Rhine. At Wiesbaden I boarded a bus to Bissersheim, where the workcamp was.

## August 9, 1953

Bissersheim was a village in the province of Der Pfalz, west of a large curve of the Rhine at the French border. Its main product was wine; vineyards surrounded the village as far as the eye could see. In the background were mountains. The houses in Bissersheim were typically German—white with brown decorative boards—and its streets were of cobblestone.

Our campers were from many countries: Sweden, Denmark, Spain, the United States, and many young men from different parts of Germany. Two of us were Finns, Helena and I. Our job was to help build a school for refugee children. First we finished digging the foundation, then worked long days with sand, gravel and cement. At this camp we actually liked our kitchen duty days, for we could get to know one another better. At the building site it was so noisy I couldn't hear anyone.

Jens was an art student from Copenhagen. He was a gentle giant, a blond Viking. He loved to draw and paint in water colors. We sifted sand for days together—he in his ski cap and I in my ski boots and beret. Somehow Jens became my shadow.

At this camp each of us had a local family of our own with whom we ate on Saturdays and Sundays. I had a family of four with two sons, ages six and eight. They were a happy family, talkative and handsome. They talked non-stop, but I didn't understand them at all; the same as in Copenhagen—whatever I said, they understood perfectly and were delighted. It took me a week to figure out their dialect, and when I did, I had no problem. My first experience with wine was that it went directly into my head which then felt heavy. To my surprise, even the children were allowed to have wine on Sundays!

In Germany: Sinikka and Jens, 1953.

## August 15, 1953

We didn't entertain the villagers since we saw them during the weekends. Often they accompanied us on our hikes and excursions, such as the boat trip to Grünstadt and Heidelberg on the Rhine. The scenery was picturesque with the castles on top of the river banks and hills. Jens immortalized them on his canvas. From a high point in Heidelberg—where the cypresses grow—we could see the old city with its winding cobblestone streets. The Rhine shone like a ribbon in the middle of the lush, green valley below us.

Many spoke German, so I had lots of practice with that language. Lothar and Gerhard were two young men who had been to war whose effects they still felt. I was so happy my German was getting better!

A note in my diary says, "I met so many good people last summer, like the old man with the sack on his back in Bissersheim. I met him on the street and greeted him saying 'Abend!' as we passed. He answered with, 'Guten Abend, Fräulein!' and stopped me. He put his sack down, bent over it, and handed me a red-cheeked, fuzzy peach." I concluded that the world was good and only a few individuals were spoiling it.

## August 20, 1953

Just before camp time ended, Bissersheim held its traditional August festival of wine, and the Burgermeister led the festivities. Since the main crop of the region was grapes, and since every house had a brewery in the basement, the wine flowed! Accordion music played through the night: "Roll out the barrels, we'll have a barrel of fun!" Colorful national costumes were worn by men, women and children—lederhosen were plentiful as were Tyrolian hats and skirts. There was dancing, eating, wine, and beer.

At one point the Burgermeister stood up, asking for silence. He thanked the campers and presented us each with two bottles of the best Rhine wine from Bissersheim. I took the bottles home to Finland.

To say good-bye to so many villagers and friends was not easy. A group of people gathered at the bus stop to see me off—giving me flowers. We hugged and cried and promised to write and meet again. Ahead of me was a train trip to Frankfurt.

## August 22, 1953

Willie from Frankfurt was a workcamper and member of KVT in Helsinki. He had come to Finland in search of work like many Germans had after the war. When he heard that I was going to Germany, he asked me to visit his parents in Frankfurt. I carried a letter and a gift to them from him. I spent the night on the train and arrived at Frankfurt in the morning. I called Willie's parents, got instructions to their home, and again was treated like a princess, fed, and entertained.

From Bissersheim I had sent a wire to Horst in northern Germany announcing that as I was on my way home, I could stop to see him. I wouldn't stop unless I heard from him. His telegram arrived, saying, "Willkommen!"

## August 24, 1953

Another night on the train. The next morning I got off at Bremen, hundreds of kilometers north of Frankfurt. There I changed trains to Oldenburg, a town not far to the west. I called Horst, who soon appeared at the station. Horst, my "Casanova" from Autiosaari, the year before! The theme for the day became my two wine bottles sticking out from the outer pockets of my knapsack. Horst thought it was the funniest thing on earth and often, when introducing me to his co-workers, also introduced my wine bottles to them. They all worked on a government refugee children's project outside Oldenberg and lived in a government housing project in town. We spent most of the day at the camp playing with children and talking with adults.

At night we drove back to town in a government car under a full moon that colored everything blue and made us quiet. We stopped to have ice cream at a little table by the window, reflecting on our day, the moon, and life. In his room we sat on the floor across from one another looking at the many pictures he had from the Autiosaari camp, and at each other. Something was said about how unbelievable it was that we were there then, and how wonderful it was. After a whole year, we said "*Gute Nacht*" to each other, forgetting everything for a moment.

## August 25, 1953

Early the next morning, Horst woke me up, and we had breakfast, saying very little. At the station, with the train ready to leave, we said, "Auf Wiedersehen . . ." and the train took me away, releasing steam that blocked my view, and making noise that drowned the farewells and quieted my pounding heart. "Auf Wiedersehen, auf Wiedersehen" rattled the train, and "This wonderful day has come to an end" sang my brain, "*Dank für die Stunden die ich bei dir hab gebunden . . .* thank you for the moments I had with you . . ." said the song. Trees, houses, flower gardens rushed by me, little by little consoling and calming me down. Copenhagen, Stockholm, and six passport checkpoints followed, and at the end of the journey was my new home at Mankkaa.

## November 1953

More than three months after my return I wrote the last chapter in my diary. In it I analyzed "*Mein Grosse Liebe*" or "My great love" as something very exciting and idyllic, and that Horst was the only Don Juan or Rhett Buttler in my life, and he enriched it a great deal.

## Fall 1953

Gray autumn days stretched from September until Christmas. Jens,

the Dane, wrote me reams of letters expressing his joy about our time in
Bissersheim. Later he seemed to fall in depression about his art studies.
The water color he had painted on our cruise on the Rhine was framed
on the wall of my room, and I looked at it often. One day I received a letter
of ten pages in Danish from Jens, and once he wrote me in Finnish!

At my work I was in distress, too, for I didn't like being stuck there.
The question "What now?" kept popping up. The fact that our home at
Mankkaa was finished happened too late. The room I had dreamed of
wasn't upstairs, and I was sharing it with Anja. It was a pleasant room with
new furniture of light-colored birch. For financial and governmental
reasons, we had to rent out the entire upstairs.

At the insurance company Katri Häggman was in charge of the ac-
counts of certain insurance inspectors. She worked in the same room with
me and others. Miss Häggman was a tiny, wiry woman in her fifties, blonde,
with frameless glasses and polished nails. She was not married and was
very efficient and mysterious in that no one knew her or her system.

## January 1954

For some time Miss Häggman had been disappearing during her lunch
hour, and when she returned, she coughed a great deal. One day she told
us not to worry, she did not have tuberculosis. Then one day she didn't
show up to work, but asked the head of our department for me to visit her.
I was to take along certain files and supplies. So I went to her home outside
the city. She patiently explained to me the whole scheme of her system that
consisted of blue and red pencil-marked numbers. I was to take her place
until she recovered. I visited her a few times, and started working overtime.
When I had learned the system, I taught my friend Raisa. The two of us
enjoyed our new job late at night with our sandwiches and fresh coffee. We
in turn taught the secrets of Miss Häggman's job to our supervisor.

Katri Häggman never returned to work, but died of cancer the following summer when I wasn't in Finland. Had I stayed, I would have had
an ideal job with a good salary and prestige. But my plans for attending a
workcamp in America had come through; I received a one-year scholarship
from the Quaker organization that would pay my return trip as well as my
upkeep. I needed to raise the rest of the money myself.

## February and March 1954

It was my busiest time ever, for Raisa and I were working long days at
the office. I was also in charge of the KVT Newsletter; some called me
Editor-in-chief. I attended most of the events KVT had and joined the
others for special get-togethers.

*Chapter 18*

# To America in 1954

**March 1954**

The scholarship I received from the American Friends Service Committee would pay for my room and board, transportation while on the North American continent, and my boat trip back. In addition, I would receive ten dollars a month for pocket money. I was advised to study Spanish, for after the summer camp I would go to a Latin American country for the rest of the year.

The spring of 1954 proved busy. To the overtime at the office and time spent on the KVT Newsletter, I added the study of Spanish to my schedule. I studied the Berlitz book by myself and found the language easy and somehow old-fashioned. I learned to conjugate the irregular verbs and practiced speaking Spanish with Armas, a fellow at KVT.

The money I earned by doing Miss Häggman's work added to my regular savings, and I soon purchased the ticket to America on a Finnish freighter. During lunch hours I hurried to the Health Department for a series of vaccinations: for typhoid on my chest, tetanus on my back next to the spine and so many others. The nurse read the instructions for shots she had never even heard of. From each shot I reacted with fever. Getting a passport and two visas—for the United States of America and Mexico—also took some running around during my lunch breaks.

**June 8, 1954**

Mother and I spent the night before my ship sailed at the Partanen's home in Kotka, about 120 kilometers east of Helsinki. They had been neighbors of ours in Värtsilä.

*Finntrader* was a brand-new, handsome Finnish freighter, transporting hundreds of tons of paper—huge rolls of newsprint—to America. The freighter also carried ten passengers, one of whom was I! During the eleven days crossing the Atlantic Ocean, I came to know the ship quite well—from the noisy engine room criss-crossed with colored pipes to the bridge. I met the first mate at the wheel and saw the radar turning on the top of the bridge and the flags and banners beating in the wind. The deck area, with its lounge chairs lined up side by side, became home to many passengers. We watched the waves and searched for whales and icebergs.

We came to know the captain and the officers, especially those who served us at the table with white gloves and starched towels hanging on their left arms. We were taken care of very well!

Tuuli, my cabin mate, was eight years old and on her way to meet one of her parents in New York. She spoke English as well as Finnish.

## June 8, 1954

Topi, a passenger I met in Copenhagen while we docked there for a short time, was a student on his way to Canada where his uncle lived. Of the other passengers I remember a man on his way to Massachusetts as an immigrant. I remember thinking how sad his situation was! Topi supposed I was also a student (with the white cap), and he called me his "Quaker girl." I spoke English better than he did. Together we studied Spanish on the deck. We spent much time together and became inseparable during those eleven long days.

We played with Tuuli and tucked her in bed every night. There was much dancing after dark. Topi hardly allowed anyone else to dance with me. We loved certain pieces of music, such as "Oh my love, my darling. . ." and "You took my heart, you took my love so tenderly . . ." We learned the words and sang and danced to the music.

A change in our routine took place when a storm hit, making *Finntrader* roll and sway. Often it felt as if we were being pushed up a steep slope, then suddenly plunged full force to the bottom of a gully, leaving us gasping and holding onto the rails. The next morning the dining room was vacant— not a soul waited for breakfast. I had a cup of black coffee.

## June 13, 1954

What *Finntrader* experienced wasn't a storm, we were told. These were left-over waves from a storm we never saw. Within twenty-four hours the sea calmed down and climbing stairs became more manageable. The lounge chairs on the deck quickly filled up with passengers wrapped in their blankets.

Our fellow passengers seeing Topi and me together all the time, first smiled at us, but as the American shore neared, they grew worried about us. During the last night on the ship, the immigrant man approached us on deck, saying that he felt someone needed to tell us that shipboard romances were dangerous, for the situation was temporary and unrealistic. Reality would hit us in America, where many adventures would be waiting. He wished us luck and asked us to believe him. We thanked him kindly, but did not believe a word he had said!

## June 19, 1954

When we heard the fog horn and the ship's bells ringing, and a commotion of ropes and tug boats around the ship began, Topi and I stood trancelike, paralyzed, holding onto each other. We had arrived at Portland, Maine! I woke to "Seneca!" coming from somewhere upstairs. Rose Perry, my friend from Camp Ruukinsalo three years before, had come to pick me up with Norma, another workcamper, whose big black car soon filled up with my shipmates. Norma drove us to Boston, where everyone got off. Good-byes and thank-yous were exchanged. There also Topi's and my path separated with a kiss and a promise: "Write to me!" "Every day!" as he boarded a train north.

The next thing I remember was that Rose and I were at the top of the Empire State Building. From there a breath-taking view of the forest of skyscrapers opened up before us. I saw ships in the harbor and the sea I had recently crossed, and I felt homesick. Rose took me to her parents' home in New Jersey for a few days. From there I traveled to Philadelphia and Pendle Hill, the Quaker institute of learning, situated in a park where people walked across a lawn to get from one class to another or sat under the trees reading or resting. I attended suggested classes and Silent Meetings. But I didn't really understand what went on. I had been on the ship for eleven days, and now was alone. Everything had changed in my life. I wasn't unhappy. It was as if I were suspended somewhere. I would need time to adjust. But new people entered my life, one of them John Flemmons from England. The two of us would travel by bus across the United States to a camp on the Navajo Indian reservation in New Mexico.

## June 25, 1954

For three days and two nights John and I sat on buses, changing countless times, and each time paying twenty-five cents for a new pillow. John was calm and quiet; he read most of the way. He traveled in Bermuda shorts and a black t-shirt and wore sandals. And he was protective of me and knew how to use a coin-operated telephone for a long distance call, retrieving a jacket I had left on one of the buses.

In June the desert in the Southwest was at its hottest, but since the summer rains had not yet started, the heat was dry and easier to take than humid heat. It was cool only on the sprinkled lawn in front of our headquarters and after sundown. We were housed in the Navajo Boarding

School's dormitories. Our job was to help build a community center for the Navajos at Crownpoint, near Gallup. I again sifted sand, a job with which I was quite familiar. I learned from our Navajo teacher to cut stone and to shape it for the foundation. I again wore my ski boots, but in place of my beret was a wide-rimmed sombrero. We ate salt tablets and saw rattle snakes daily. "It's bloody hot," said John one day.

The camp leaders were Paul and Mona Dayton from Oregon, who had their four children with them. The Daytons seemed a typical American family: cheerful, handsome, individualistic, daring and wasteful! Paul, a tall man in his forties, loved the company of young people. Mona was warm and motherly. There were many young American campers; John and I were the only foreigners. All were eager, well-groomed, individualistic and talented.

Hearing so many people speaking English differently, I started noticing dialects. There was much kidding about the different ways of speaking and of customs each state had. Sitting on fine Navajo rugs in the living room, we sang to the accompaniment of one of the guitar players. I learned tens of American folksongs, such as "Sweet Betsy from Pike," "Oh Shenandoah, I love to hear you . . .," and "Oh, give me a home where the buffalo roam . . ." Singing was a good way of escaping homesickness, for, as soon as the evening shadows grew and the sun sank behind the purple mesa, I was filled with a longing I knew already in Värtsilä as a child.

At the camps in Finland I had noticed that Americans loved to have discussions. But I couldn't understand how they dared talk when they didn't seem to know anything about the issue at hand! In Finland they wanted to discuss the idea of a united Europe! Decades later I learned about "brain storming," a technique used in schools and workshops in America. In brainstorming, the ideas of different speakers are listed, categorized, discussed, eliminated, voted on, and the kernel of a valuable thought may be found! How about the idea of a united Europe now—more than three decades later?

During our lunch break, in the heat of the mid-day sun, I usually walked through the sandy landscape to the Trading Post, where the Navajos sold silver and turquoise jewelry, leather goods, sand paintings, and beautiful rugs. Food could be bought also, and the mail came there. Most of the Navajo women dressed in stunning Gypsy-like dresses of colorful silk and velvet. Some of them, and most of the men, spoke English.

## June-August 1954

I lived on Topi's daily letters while adjusting to life in the desert. Letters from my family and friends arrived also, so I was happy. I promptly answered all those letters, for I needed to feel attached, safe. I was learning to eat new foods: peanut butter on celery and tuna fish salad between two pieces of bread. I drank lukewarm water from the canteen and watched my steps for rattlers. I learned to appreciate Clorox as a stain remover and taking my time in doing things. I was strong and loved physical work.

## July 2, 1954

I soon found that distances are enormous in America, and that Americans were used to them, even if they came from the eastern states. They were used to traveling! Although the desert landscape looked barren with many cacti on it, it held a charm in its pastel-colored, eternal mountains fringing the openness. I enjoyed the star-lit skies and cool nights as we lay watching and listening in our sleeping bags under the trees. Since most animals came out only at night (not the snakes that liked it hot), it was exciting to hear their sounds.

One night a thunder shower surprised us, and in the morning our vehicles got stuck in the mud. We scurried around, carrying rocks to put under the wheels, and waited until the sun came out and dried the roads.

## July 6, 1954

One day Lynn and I joined the young hospital doctor, Jan, who wasn't much older than we were, help a Navajo boy. A telephone call from a remote area of the reservation reported that a seven-year-old boy had been bitten by a rattle snake. Jan drove the hospital vehicle, a jeep stripped of its back seat, over the ruts of the dusty road while Lynn and I bounced around and bumped against the metal walls of the "ambulance." We were to meet a truck bringing the boy to us.

When we saw the boy, he was unconscious. His arm was swollen and blue. When the boy was placed in our vehicle, the doctor listened to his heart, gave him an anti-venom injection, cleaned the arm and made a cross cut on the bite. She drew blood from the wound with a suction cup, and put water on the boys lips, instructing Lynn and me that we were to do that the rest of the way. She drove since we didn't know how.

We fastened the boy's stretcher with leather straps onto hooks on the floor. At intervals, we pumped blood from the wound. We wiped the boy's face and kept moistening his lips. We adjusted his position, and cushioned his arm when the road got very bumpy. The boy groaned. Even if he had been conscious, he wouldn't have spoken with us; his language was Navajo.

## July 9, 1954

The boy was well enough to leave the hospital after a few days. When Lynn and I went to see him, his dark eyes were wide open, and his white pillow was covered by the black profusion of his long hair.

Both Navajo men and women had long, black hair, mostly held in a ponytail rather than loose or braided. Their facial features were strong and serene, and their costumes, earrings, necklaces and rings were beautiful. Many wore jewelry all the time.

During weekends workcampers took trips to historic places, such as to Mesa Verde National Park in southwestern Colorado, where we saw the magnificent cliff dwellings built by the Pueblo Indians. We also saw the round ruins and Kivas of Chaco Canyon in northwestern New Mexico.


## August 30, 1954

My time at the Crownpoint camp came to an end, and, early one morning, our leader, Paul, drove me to El Paso, Texas, where I would cross the border to Mexico. In El Paso we ate a very spicy lunch, an introduction of spiciness to come, as Paul put it. He had been coaching me about Mexico and Mexican ways, which he loved. He spoke Spanish well, which he and I had been practicing at camp while working. He gave me seventy-five dollars for my travel expenses from Friends Service Committee's funds.

After saying good-bye to Paul, I walked the short distance to the Mexican border, while the music of "Vaya con Dios, my darling, vaya con Dios, my love," echoed in the streets, touching my heart with memories of someone with whom I had been singing it on the ship that brought us across the Atlantic. The sun shone brightly as I read the schedule of departures outside the Mexican bus depot. I chose the bus that left the soonest toward the south and my destination, Mexico City. The price of $6.25 seemed low to me; later I was to know why. The most exciting trip of my life had begun!

# Chapter 19

# Mexico!

**August 30, 1954**

On my first afternoon on the Mexican bus, brown-skinned people with bundles of all sorts got on and off continuously. They seemed to know each other, for everyone greeted everyone as they climbed on board and politely asked permission to go through the narrow aisle with their burdens, occasionally bumping into those sitting along their way. They smiled and laughed while speaking their musical language of which I understood some words.

I sat down on the first empty seat, next to an older man who made room for me. Soon he picked and strummed his guitar. The only Mexican song I knew was "Cielito Lindo," which my father sang in Finnish. "Ay, ay, ay, ay, your beautiful eyes are shining!" ("Ai, ai, ai, ai, katsees' kaunis hohtaa" . . .) When I began to sing it, the old man's brown eyes lit up with pleasure.

At each bus stop, herds of food peddlers surrounded the bus with food baskets and noise, trying to outdo each other. People hung out the window, buying all kinds of foods whose smells filled the bus, strange smells and new foods for me. I didn't dare touch them. I had been warned about bacteria and stomach illness. In fact, the only food I ate during the entire 2,500 kilometer trip, was an apple given me by a fellow passenger.

Anything seemed to be allowed on the bus, even pigs that were stuffed into the net above our heads and chicken tied in bundles with other chickens. There was a turkey next to me, its head down and its eyes blinking in fright. Its owner held it by the legs while standing in the aisle. There were fat baskets, bright-colored bags, mothers with swinging earrings and then children, and men with blankets on their shoulders and sombreros on their heads.

My first problem was a rest room. Once, when we stopped in a village, I stepped out and followed the line to the bathroom. I had not even reached the place, when I turned around, holding my breath, and rushed away! The

driver saw me, understood, and told me he would take care of me. And he
did! He stopped at each hotel for me to use the rest room. I was grateful
but had to put a stop to the stopping, saying: "No gracias, señor!"

The view from the bus window was similar to New Mexico—desert
and yuccas standing straight like candles. It changed only in the evening
when the mountain ranges became dark silhouettes against the sinking
sun. Seemingly identical, dimly-lit villages passed by. Music played everywhere! It was happy and encouraged me.

The chatter quieted, then stopped altogether as the bus darkened, and
the heads of the people leaned back. It was actually cozy in there, when
the only sound was that of the tires on the road below us. Even the driver
with his dangling rosary beads became a dark silhouette, just like the Sierra
Madre mountains, which seemed to follow us. Stars twinkled in the familiar
constellations of the northern hemisphere but strangely tilted on their
sides.

The peace of the moment was broken by me, however, when I went to
the driver, my dictionary in hand. He turned the lights on and stopped the
bus as I tried to read my first Spanish sentence—about someone leaning
against me. He understood at least the word "molesta," turned around and
looked at the man, and said something to the people behind him. They
moved to the back, and I was motioned to occupy their seat.

The night passed, another day dawned, people got off and new ones
got on. The trip just kept going on! I began to understand why it was so
cheap; this was the third class bus that stopped anywhere and for anything!
We stopped all the time! I should have taken a first class bus. How long
would this trip take? At least the driver seemed to understand what I meant.
He lifted his hand with five fingers. I thought that was a good sign: five
minutes, and began to take my bags down. "No, señorita, cinco horas más!"
he said, and I realized he had meant five hours more.

I let myself back down into the seat, sighing. He smiled consolingly.
When he got tired, another driver, who had been sleeping in the back, took
over the driving.


## September 3, 1954

At last, after three days and two nights, one morning early we arrived
in Mexico City at a terminal I later was unable to find. It was a hole in the
wall, and most of the passengers flowed over to the room next door, which
had new grave stones! I sat on one, just like the others did, wrapped in my
plastic raincoat for warmth, until seven o'clock, when I called the Casa de
los Amigos, the Quaker headquarters, on Calle Campeche.

Florence, the hostess, answered the telephone and advised me to take
a taxi, which I did—costing only ten pesos. At the Casa I soon found myself
at a round table eating papaya with lemon, oatmeal with milk and bananas,

and having a delicious cup of coffee after such a long journey! After breakfast I was shown my bunkbed and the shower. I was in heaven!

## September 4, 1954

I slept for twenty hours. I had reached my limit for new experiences, and I didn't want any more at the moment. I just wanted to be left alone. They finally made me get up, and I ended up going to see a bullfight the next day. I got to know two jolly English girls, Joice and Bunty, with whom I traveled in the back of a truck to Ixmiquilpan, a town about 150 kilometers northeast of Mexico City.

Sinikka and hosts' children, 1954.

*Chapter 20*

# With the Otomi Indians

## September 1954

Ixmiquilpan was a typical Mexican town in the state of Hidalgo, 150 kilometers northeast of Mexico City, with a few thousand inhabitants, mostly Otomi Indians. The Otomis had been pushed back by more aggressive tribes hundreds of years before and had settled in the high-altitude Mesquital Valley, surrounded by mountains. Since the rainfall was low, the vegetation consisted mostly of cacti, among them "pipe organ" cactus that bore berries. Mesquite trees, slow-growing hardwoods, also grow there. Pepper trees with red berries grew next to houses. The main crops are corn, beans, and magueyes (agave), which produced, among other things, a beverage rich in vitamin C called *agua miel* or honey water. When fermented, it became a foamy, beer-like drink.

The daytime temperature was often hot due to the cloudless skies. For the same reason, the nights were cool, freezing in the winter. The saying, "One gets burned in the sun and freezes in the shade," just about describes the climate.

The center of the town was typical of Mexican towns, for it had a "plaza," a square that consisted of a park with a round, ornate bandstand. Paths departed from the bandstand, like rays of light, to all parts of the park. Huge trees, whose trunks were painted white to a meter high, gave comfortable shade to the flowers and bushes, as well as to the people strolling there or sitting on the benches. The streets surrounding the plaza were the busiest in town, for all government offices, such as the post office and the police department were there. The main church or cathedral, like a caring mother, stood there, too, its bells calling people for worship many times a day.

In an unbroken wall, houses of different colors followed the narrow sidewalks. The bottoms of the houses, up to a meter high, were painted a darker color; the rest of the walls were white, yellow, pink, blue or orange.

Harsh advertisements usually took over the store fronts and the walls. A sturdy double door made of wood or metal led to the center patio, which was also the garden. It was surprising to me to see the patio with so many lovely flowers, often a fountain, and colorful birds chirping in the cages, when the street was so ugly. The rooms of houses opened to the patio, their doors serving as windows.

The stores in the portico were squeezed together, and loud music echoed from the ceiling. People came and went, carrying baskets, the women covering their heads with dark *rebozos*—for shade from the sun—and the men with their sombreros pulled down toward their eyes.

Bunty, Joice and I were like giants when standing among local people, who were short, stocky, and sunburned. We found the address of our camp headquarters, knocked on the door and were led down a narrow corridor of hanging plants, arriving at the patio. It had a typical open water tank (*la pila*) and a slanted washtub made of concrete. Many colorful hanging plants surrounded it. The door to the camp kitchen stood open. A piece of bright blue sky arched above us.

## September 3, 1954

We soon got to know two Americans, Kater and Hilda. Later Hilda pulled out her recorder and played a Mexican song she had taught herself: "Qué lejos estoy del suelo donde he nacido . . ." ("How far away I am from the land of my birth.") It compared a person to a leaf in the wind and was very emotional in its melody and lyrics. The song seemed to fit me very well, for I had not received any mail since leaving Crownpoint, New Mexico.

Our first purpose was to get to know the local Health Department and to help with their work. At one meeting we attended, we learned that our job would be to vaccinate people against smallpox and to get rid of the fleas and lice they might have with DDT-powder. The young doctor told us about his immediate plan to tour some mountain villages for a week, setting up a clinic each day in a different village. He asked for two volunteers to accompany him and his four nurses on the trip. After a few silent moments I raised my hand, and Bunty followed me!

## September 4, 1954

The next afternoon seven of us got in the back of a truck with our supplies and were driven to the end of the road. From there we walked to the nearest village for the night. The climb wasn't easy. We followed the edge of a canyon, a steep slope, carrying supplies for a week. When two local men offered Bunty and me their horses, we jumped at the idea, although neither of us was a horsewoman. But even my remembered terror of a previous ride didn't keep me from taking him up on his offer. Night suddenly fell, and we couldn't see a foot ahead! We were afraid the horses would take a wrong step, and that would have meant falling into the ravine! My horse seemed in a hurry to get home, so he pulled ahead hard, leaving everyone behind. There I was, alone on a strange horse, in the mountains of Mexico, at the edge of canyon! I kept calling for Bunty, and she called to me. I could hear her asking, "Luz, señor, por favor!" ("Light, please, sir!") We learned from that trip that one can trust a horse.

I remember only two of the six nights we spent in the Sierra Madre Mountains. The first one was spent in a small room, all of us side by side like sardines in a can. In the morning we were itchy with flea bites. The second night we slept outdoors under a rickety ramada used by the chickens. They preferred the roof; we were subject to bombing raids!

Early in the morning we set up the clinic, some of us helping the doctor, others vaccinating and dusting people's hair with our white powder. This we repeated on six mornings. The most common cases of sickness I saw were coughs, colds, and diarrhea in children. There were also eye infections, broken bones and fever cases. Bunty and I learned to vaccinate and to say, "No duele." ("It doesn't hurt.") At every chance the nurses taught us more Spanish . . . and more love songs, which we sang as we walked between villages and at night. One of them was: "Tú eres como una espinita que se me ha clavado en el corazón, suave que me estás, sangrando que me estás, matando de dolor!" ("You are like a thorn that has pierced my heart, and you are slowly bleeding me, killing me with pain!")

The doctor, Bunty and I were dressed and equipped for the excursion. The nurses wore white, rather long and full nurses' dresses, boots and sombreros, their black braids swinging against their backs from under the wide-brimmed hats. They were very young, trained nurses.

## September 5, 1954

On the second day I began to feel nauseous and weak. Because I didn't like the beans that were part of every meal, I had not eaten enough. (My dislike of beans went back to wartime Helsinki, when Juhani, Kerttu and I ate some bean seeds that had been treated with poison and were meant for planting only. That day, on our way back from Haaga where we had the vegetable plots, the three of us were hanging over the edge of the street car, vomiting and hurting badly.)

That afternoon with the sun beating hard, I stayed behind, stopping to rest more than the others. I didn't think I was able to go any higher, when someone called from above describing a lovely green meadow. I decided to make it up there before resting. The meadow came with high-grade bulls (for bullfighting), though, so resting was not possible. My disappointment was great. When the doctor heard about my situation, he took a can of shrimp from his backpack, opened it and made me drink the juice. I did and recovered for the rest of the "tour!" And I ate beans from then on and learned to like them, too.

School children at Cuesta.

When we reached a fork in the path, we saw a sign on a tree that warned anybody of coming to the village. They had cases of smallpox there. We skipped that village, but hit all the rest of them. I don't recall ever washing up during that trip. We used alcohol for cleansing our hands and the places on the arms where we placed the vaccine. We drank boiled water.

## September 10, 1954

When we finally "were finished with the mountain," Bunty's good humor returned, and we felt happy and relieved. We found things to joke about—even about the doctor's "harem"—for there were six women around him at that moment, resting under a tree. As we entered the plain, we thought we were seeing a mirage ahead of us: a Pepsi Cola sign on the wall of a hut. But as we entered, there was cool Pepsi for drinking! I have never appreciated or enjoyed any drink as much as that!

Bunty and I eagerly anticipated a hot bath, fresh fruit and a pile of mail upon our arrival at the camp, but we found the kitchen and the whole house totally empty. After the shock wore off, we headed toward the house of the head of the Health Department, and that's where we found everyone. Some were swimming in a sparkling pool, others tanning themselves or sipping soda. No one jumped up with open arms to greet us! We stood there in dismay, tired and dusty.

The shower washed the six-day dirt off us quickly, and as we returned to the patio, a surprise awaited us: the table had been set for a feast, and everybody shouted: "Surprise! Welcome back!" And they hugged us and asked questions. When I asked about my mail, they said none had come. They even checked the matter and were sorry. So was I; how could it be?

Another surprise waited for me at home. It was a bundle of thirteen letters tied together with a ribbon! When the others had seen that many of my letters were from the same person, Topi, they had decided to play a trick on me.

Chapter 21

# In the Tropics, 1954

**September 11, 1954**

After the exhausting week on the mountains of Hidalgo, where we vaccinated hundreds of people against smallpox, I returned to Mexico City and the "Casa" with the others. From there we traveled to Camomila, Morelos, an hour's ride south, to attend the winter workcamp orientation conference. We heard inspiring speakers such as Heberto Sein, a philosopher and a marvelous orator. Red-haired Heberto was in his sixties. He remembered everyone's name. (I was always "Silvia" to him, for "Sinikka" or "Cínica" in Spanish meant "cynical.") Among others, we also met Jean and Ed Duckles, who had been guiding the workcamp movement for years, and knew Mexico and the Mexican way of living very well.

**September 12, 1954**

One evening after supper at the Casa, as I sat and talked, I noticed a well-dressed young man drying dishes, singing sentimental songs as he put them in the china cabinet. He had an aquiline nose that suited his face, dark hair and skin. He was short and serious-looking. I found out he was a Mexican workcamper by the name of Agustín García de la Rosa, soon to become extremely important in my life.

We learned many aspects of workcamps in Mexico and met people from all over the world. Bunty, Joice, Hilda, John (who had come down from Crownpoint) and I would be going to Zaragoza in Veracruz, a semitropical state. Also in our group were: Tony, who had a large black car, Bruce, Pete, Sandy, Lyle, Kirstin, Francis, Cecilia, Lee, Elsa, and Agustín. Our camp leaders were Gino and Eunice Baumann. Of nineteen campers, eleven were Americans. Of the new people, Elsa and Gino were from Switzerland, Kirstin from Denmark, and Agustín from Mexico. We had become more international!

Most of the American boys were C.O.s or "conscientious objectors," who had volunteered for workcamp work for two years in place of bearing arms and going to war. They were pacifists and paid for their room and board.

## September 13, 1954

In Tony's black car or the back of a truck some of us traveled to Zaragoza, a long day's journey from the altitude of 2,400 meters to near sea level. The scenery of agaves changed to that of banana trees, and noticeably the temperature rose.

Zaragoza was a lush, green village with muddy streets and vividly colored bouganvillas in the plaza. The daily rain shower had just finished when we arrived, and water still dripped from the roof of our house. Many children called Agustín's name, for he had spent his previous camp there.

The front part of the house consisted of a large main room, the kitchen, the girls' dormitory, the camp leader's room, and an extra room. Two large doors opened to the street and served also as windows. A door also led to the patio, at the edge of which was the boys' dormitory, and the outhouse under two tall palm trees.

The house, made of bricks plastered and white-washed, had floors of concrete painted terra cotta. The high ceilings were supported by wooden beams. The people of Zaragoza showed a lighter complexion than the Otomis in Hidalgo. Their eyes were lighter brown, and some had green

Top left: Bruce, Sandy, Saul and Howie. Bottom: Chico, John, Tony, and Lyle, 1954.

Zaragoza Camp, 1954.

eyes also. The economy was based on agriculture: two generous crops of corn per year, sugar cane, fruits, coffee on the hills, and vanilla.

One of the first things for us to do was form committees. The kitchen crew did the planning, shopping, preparation and preservation of food. They also served food and washed the dishes. Each camper in a group of three, served for a week. The central committees formed subcommittees that set work plans, communicated with the village leaders and with the Friends Service Committee in Philadelphia. Agustín was our most important link with the community, for he could sense and communicate feelings, reactions, and wishes of each party; he was our liason. Gino and Bruce spoke some Spanish and were brave enough to use it. To improve our Spanish, we held classes in the evenings; we had discovered that each effort to speak Spanish was much appreciated by the community. Each morning after breakfast, we gathered for a Silent Meeting, which always ended with Gino kissing Eunice lightly on her lips—as if to say "Amen."

## September 14, 1954

According to my notes, our first morning in the village was noisy: a neighbor had slaughtered a pig early that morning. Not only did the pig lament its fate, but the turkeys, burros, and dogs did. This was early September. The afternoon shower that had brought relief from the heat hadn't stopped, but continued for four days. We found the sound of rain on our tin roof much more to our liking than the scurrying of rats, but we found mold in our shoes in the morning.

The men's work consisted of digging a ditch from a spring many kilometers away to the center of Zaragoza. Water pipes would be laid in the ditch, and fresh, clean water would be brought to a faucet in the plaza. The work was hard because of the heat. One of the women took refreshments to the men each day. One of us also did their laundry. Since pretty Cecilia liked both jobs, we generally let her do them. She also drove our truck to Martínez de la Torre, the nearest town, for shopping; the villagers were surprised at her talent, since women didn't drive in Mexico in 1954.

Every morning most of the women in our group went to Misantla, a town in the opposite direction from Martínez, to work with the Health Department in their vaccination program. One day Francis and I vaccinated 150 children against smallpox. The "No duele" phrase that Bunty and I had learned in Ixmiquilpan came in handy again and was used at least 150 times that day. Later, some of us were taught how to immunize people against diphtheria, whooping cough and tetanus, which was done by injecting in the arm with a syringe. I also learned to give injections of penicillin into the tough muscles of the buttocks. I preferred smallpox vaccination, though. It only involved cleaning an area with alcohol, pricking the skin of the arm, and emptying the contents of a tiny vial under the skin.

With my clever friend Hilda, we started a kindergarten program for the little kids of the village. As soon as this was going well, we started a library in our spare room. For the kindergarten we found an abandoned building; a roof, pillars that supported it and two walls. This was a place for drying vanilla in the rainy season.

Hilda and I also started intense study of Spanish, each night writing down our plans for the next day's kindergarten, checking it with Agustín. We also learned several children's songs and dances, and gathered materials. We even sent for finger puppets from the United States, using cereal box offers. When we presented our ideas to the group, they liked them, but when we asked for volunteers from the boys' group, only John Flemmons seemed willing.

## September 13, 1954

For the library, we designed a lending system with file cards for some fifty books, mostly classics, such as *Caperucita Roja* (*Little Red Riding Hood*). Library hours were in the afternoon, when it often was raining. The children could stay and read, or take the book home.

A note in my diary says: "I talked Spanish for two hours this morning in the kindergarten, where John and I played with twenty children. We were kept busy! John drew pictures for the kids, and I danced circle dances with them, such as: "Naranja dulce, limón partido, dame un abrazo que yo te pido . . ."

I must mention that from Mexico City I had written Topi a description of my adventure on the mountains of Ixmiquilpan. In return I had received a hasty offer from him: to leave "that savage place" and go to Canada where he was. His uncle would pay for my trip. I wrote him back, thanking him— but no, I had never run away from my duty, nor after a man, and wouldn't do it now! I confessed not being a student (with the white cap and the golden lyre), which he had assumed, and which I had let him believe.

## September 14, 1954

In the middle of September my diary tells about how sleepy I was getting after the library hour had ended and the children had gone home. I read a long letter from my friend Magi in Finland, in which she told about her trip to Lapland, and of being under the spell of nature. I was wondering, under what spell I was at the moment. I had the feeling I would not be hearing from Topi again, yet it really didn't matter anymore. I had Agustín now in my thoughts.

Bruce had been given the title "Don Bruce," because he was very out-going and did a lot of public relations work among the villagers. He also appeared in his long, blanket-like cape, sombrero and sandals in the eve-nings. Ladies liked him! He taught us Spanish and Mexican music, which he accompanied with his guitar. That night Lee would be serenaded by the boys. We'd all sing "Las Mañanitas" to her, for it was her birthday. My notes also say that Agustín looked tired, for he had been on kitchen duty all week. He spent his evenings playing his guitar and singing melancholy songs, which we all were learning and liking. I enjoyed sitting by him.

One of the several guitar players we had was Sandy Darlington, who became a good friend to me. He was very sensitive, suffered headaches, was creative and loved to write. He loved everything about Mexico. Sandy had freckles and red hair, which he covered with a sombrero. He constantly tried to hide from the sun, always squinting one eye behind his glasses.

## September 15, 1954

"Our generator works for three to four hours a night. After that we burn oil lamps until they get so sooty we can't see. Poor kitchen crew; they must wash the lamps' chimneys the next day! It's cozy and comfortable. I only wish for more mail. I'm always longing for something," I wrote in my Mexican diary.

## September 16, 1954

On the sixteenth of September, we awoke to the clanging of the school bell. It was Mexico's Independence Day. "At six o'clock we found ourselves standing, half asleep and our arms folded, on the school yard. The hoisting of the green, white and red flag was taking place to the tune of Don Bruce's trumpet. He played the Mexican national anthem 'Mexicanos al grito de guerra,' and the school children sang it with vigor and enthusiasm four times through. The moon looked down on us, as did the two coconut palms from the other side of the wall. The flag, sliding slowly along the leaning flagpole, reached the top, and the firecrackers drew lines on the moon against the brightening morning sky. The atmosphere was so impressive that we woke up."

## September 19, 1954

A note in my diary tells of Howard and me serving as the steering committee and of laboring on the report with seven copies to be sent to the Philadelphia office.

One evening I showed my photographs to Agustín, now known as "Chico." He mused about my always writing "newspapers," meaning long letters. During a group trip to the large city of Puebla, he took me to his uncle's house for lunch. I met his Uncle José and his wife Tía Petrita. Chico asked permission to see my eyes. Later he sang about the green, divine eyes of a pilgrim, who came from the land of ice. It is a true song! Hand in hand we stepped into a church where a little boy kissed the statue of the Virgin Mary. Loud speakers on the street played, "Doctor, do not extract my tooth because I'll die of pain," a cha-cha tune, as we walked to join the rest of our friends. During our return trip to Zaragoza, in the back of a camper-truck, we all huddled under an army blanket because it was cold.

## September 28, 1954

I appreciated the warmth of Zaragoza after our return from the highland Puebla. Kirstin left us and so did Bunty, whose legs broke out in a ferocious rash. My skin was better than ever.

## October 4, 1954

One day we took an excursion to Papantla's pyramids at El Tajín. It was raining hard, and we waded across a deep, turbulent stream—up to our waists in rushing water. For umbrellas we used huge leaves that resembled rhubarb, but much larger. On the way back I got a horse to do the wading for me.

## October 15, 1954

At times I read St. Paul's letters during the quiet hours, searching for peace. Something disquieting had grown inside me; it had much to do with Chico.

## October 31, 1954

For the Día de Todos Santos, (All Saints Day) I helped Flora, our hostess, wrap up tamales in banana leaves. The dead were remembered with candles and food placed on altars in the corner of every home and at cemeteries. We were inundated with food that the villagers brought, and were invited to visit everyone. Chico and I made many visits together.

## November 1954

Many evenings were spent sitting with the village youngsters around our long table, playing board games, and learning new songs.

On another excursion we were all lying on the beach of Tampico, at the Gulf of Mexico. Chico and I wrote in the sand, "I love you!" as we sipped coconut milk through a straw directly from the coconut. That night we danced and danced. The next day at the camp, after a slide show on the school yard, Chico came to help me with the dishes, and he kissed me on the cheek.

## December 12, 1954

It was December, the nights were much cooler. At the plaza we cele-brated the successful completion of our drinking water project with the governor of the state of Veracruz, the mayors of the nearby towns and all the other dignitaries. The mayor of Zaragoza turned the faucet on, and toasts were made with champagne and pictures taken.

## December 20, 1954

The project finished, packing and loading started. Chico and I got a small space on the first truck among the camp furniture and dishes. We were sad after saying good-bye to everyone, and sad because we would soon be going different ways, too. Chico would, however, come for a visit in Ixmilquilpan, where I would return after the holidays. We left behind the romantic tropics and sensed the change in climate, clinging to each other. Our moment in the sun ended with singing about tropical nights and harvest moons. In a few hours we reached Huamantla, Chico's hometown in the highlands of Tlaxcala. There Chico got off and introduced all of us to his mother at the bakery. Many of us had already met her at the camp one day; she came to see Chico when he was ill. She looked surprised and very worried.

*Chapter 22*

# Winter Camp 1955

### Christmas 1954

I spent my first Christmas away from home at the Casa de los Amigos in Mexico City, in the company of many workcamp volunteers and staff members. John, Kater and Sandy were among them; together we would go to Ixmiquilpan in January. We spent Christmas Eve with an American family, singing Christmas carols by the fire. Just as we returned to the Casa, the phone rang, and I knew it would be for me. It was Chico wishing me a Merry Christmas and telling me he missed me. I told him about our plans to go to the midnight Mass; he said he would do the same.

Many of us had been to Ixmiquilpan before, but not to the new camp headquarters at the center of town, across from the cathedral. It was a concrete house with many uncozy rooms, but it had a pleasant patio. *Pirú* trees provided shade and softened the glaring white walls enclosing the patio. For privacy one could climb to the flat roof.

We divided into small groups and often met only on weekends. Some would continue vaccinating the people of the nearby villages; others would work in town. We had a kindergarten program and a library program. There were so many of us, that I didn't get to know everyone well. Kater, Jed, and I were sent to the farthest of villages, Cuesta Colorada, high in the mountains, where we would spend the week. We left on Monday mornings and returned on Saturdays. Jed was a student of agriculture, experienced in soil conservation. Kater and I were "trained" nurses, which may have been the reason we were chosen to go to the remotest village.

### December 27, 1954

We packed our sleeping bags and food for the week on Sunday night. The next morning we were dropped off at the end of a road, from where

95

we started a seven-hour guided climb. On reaching the ridge of the mountain, we could see dwellings on the inside slopes; we had arrived at a village by the name of Gundho. At the school we met some government workers, among them Elena, who sang all the time, and a young volunteer, Dick, who had devised a loom and taught weaving. The school was located at the edge of the mountain; one step too far would have been dangerous. On the other side of the school stretched a flat space where the school children played. For two days we rested at Gundho and became acclimated to the altitude. We accompanied Elena on her house visits and were starting to learn a few words in the Otomi language, "*Queashauah,*" being the most useful one, and the only one I still remember. It was a greeting used frequently: "Good morning, afternoon, evening!"

Four miles farther north, at the end of the path, was Cuesta Colorada, where we spent five months among maguey fields and the mountain tops—watching the clouds go by in the canyon below.

## January 1955

The inhabitants of the region were Otomi Indians, who were quiet, tolerant and content in their mountainous world. Only one of the women in the village spoke Spanish; she was Porfiria and had worked as a maid in Mexico City. She became our closest friend, and we visited her many times. She always invited us in, away from the hot midday sun. We often found her making corn tortillas, sitting on her heels on the dirt floor and clapping a small amount of dough between her hands until it was round and thin. She would carefully place it on the *comal* or hot plate on the fire in the middle of the floor. Turning the tortillas over, when done she placed them inside a towel in the tortilla basket to keep them warm.

Once she peeled two boiled eggs, broke each into a tortilla, added a little salt, wrapped the tortilla around it, and handed each of us one of her delicious "tacos"! To make it spicier, she offered us "salsa" of green chile peppers.

The dwellings were made of sticks and branches and used long-stemmed grass for the roof that often touched the ground. The floor was packed dirt. Other than being low, the huts were cozy with all the important utensils displayed on the walls. The patios were surrounded by fences of sticks, branches and maguey plants. Chickens ran around. Some families also kept goats, burros, and pigs. Among the animals played the uncombed, runny-nosed children, who, during the day, wore no pants. The lack of water grew worse as summer approached; no rain had fallen since the previous May. What water existed was for cooking and drinking. The laundry could wait. To hike to the bottom of the ravine took time and, in May, to fill a *cántaro* or oval earthen jug with water (five gallons) took a half hour. The water trickled down the creek on green beard-like algae and had to be boiled before use. We did what the local people did—carried the jug by attaching it with a band around the head and resting it on the back. The jug was heavy, and the path up the ravine was steep and narrow.

Rain, when it came, was heavy and destructive and, at the same time, essential to life.

Jed often had another young volunteer with him, making terraces and planting magueys to stabilize the soil on the steep, cultivated slopes. The summer rains were so heavy that they robbed fields of their top soil as the water rushed down the hillside, forming arroyos of brown water.

Kater and I got acquainted with the women and taught them about hygiene. Not as dramatic as Jed's work, our job wasn't easy because we didn't speak the language. Many times I would have preferred sifting sand, as in many earlier camps, over the slow process of social work. However, teaching crocheting and knitting to school girls and helping the school teacher, *maestro*, with recreational activities, gave me satisfaction.

Our purpose was to live on the same level with the people; we didn't eat meat for that reason. We cooked beans—at the elevation of 9,000 feet or more, it took the whole day to soften them. We bought tortillas and eggs from the villagers and ate a lot of peanut butter for protein. We ate chocolate bars while climbing, and we always had oranges with us. Each week we learned to pack a lighter and lighter backpack and were able to cut travel time from seven to two hours. We used an *ayate*, or a bag woven of maguey fibers, with a broad band for carrying it either around your forehead or as a shoulder bag.

We had a hut of our own near the school. There we cooked on an open fire, took our meals, sat around and talked at night. Jed slept there also. Kater and I placed our cots and sleeping bags in the school room and locked the doors for the night. In the morning, we knew it was time to get up when we saw people with round sombreros staring at us through the windows.

Most of the men of the village spoke some Spanish; they were the ones who went to market in Ixmiquilpan. The talk was about the upcoming rain, without which their *milpas* wouldn't grow, nor would their beans, squash, or other vegetables. The women took care of the home and the children and embroidered lovely blouses and handbags. They wove the ayate material with maguey fibers. The men did the trading; exchanging their wives' work for necessary items, such as tools and fabrics. They worked the soil and the maguey, and took care of the animals. They made sandals, the kind we also wore. It wasn't unusual to see Otomi men spinning yarn, turning the spool in their left hand and working the wool from the basket with their right hand—and helping the process with their mouths. This they did while walking on the paths between villages or when standing in groups, talking.

The Otomis couldn't survive without the ever-present maguey (agave) plant—just like the Lapps couldn't live without their reindeer. Maguey produced delicious and vitamin-rich *agua miel*, or honey water for the children, and it could be fermented into a beer-like *pulque* for the grown-ups. The maguey provided fiber and needles, as well as membranes useful for wrapping. It also produced worms, a delicacy sold for a good price on the market. The magueys were "milked" twice a day like cows and lasted for six months. When they died, they became firewood. "Unmilked" magueys lasted much longer.

On Saturdays we hurried to get down off the mountain. We could hardly wait to take a bath and read our mail! Where we had been dropped off, we were also picked up by a camper truck which took us home, covering us with a thick layer of road dust in the process.

With water scarce in Ixmiquilpan after a year without rain, it had to be rationed for baths. The men came up with a shower system which functioned thus: The gas burner on top of the shower booth on the patio heated the bucket of water. The water was coaxed down into the shower head by tugging on a string attached to the person's big toe. Each person was allowed a certain number of tugs. It was wise to wet and soap up with only one tug and save the rest for rinsing.

We often felt we didn't get enough free time on the weekends. Once in awhile even Kater, Jed and I spent the weekend in the kitchen peeling vegetables, cooking and doing dishes. Once the large pressure cooker full of beans exploded on us, plastering beans on all surfaces of the kitchen and making the floor dangerous for walking!

Since the beginning, we all wore local garb: sombreros, sandals with blankets for the men and *rebozos* (shawls) and Otomi blouses for the women. We tried to be indistinguishable from the local people, without success.

## February 1955

In the winter Chico arrived for a visit, and we took him to Cuesta Colorada with us for the whole week. It was splendid under the starry skies after the day's work was done and we could dream together. There Chico engraved "Sinikka y Agustín" on a huge maguey leaf.

## March 1955

One week while suffering an allergy attack, I stayed home, but, when word reached us about Kater being ill in Gundho, I went along with medicine and to bring her down. We mounted her on a small donkey and somehow managed the dark but familiar route with the help of flashlights.

During one of the weekends I helped Sandy's infected toe with penicillin shots; one of them was due at midnight, just at the moment when someone shouted: "A scorpion!"

## April 1955

One night Sandy and I made an appointment with the *padre* or priest of the cathedral. We entered through the back and knocked on the heavy door. The padre had just returned, dressed in a black leather outfit and a motorcycle helmet. He traveled everywhere on his motorcycle. He was a young, good-looking Italian who enjoyed our company. That night he took us to his quarters upstairs, then poured some wine for each of us. We drank for God's guidance, and until past midnight sat discussing the Catholic religion, Mexico, Chico and me, and the possible difficulties of a marriage between a Lutheran and a Catholic. He gave me no encouragement.

## May 1955

In May, Sandy and I said goodbye to our workcamp friends and, dressed in our Otomi gear of sombreros and sandals, traveled from Ixmiquilpan to Huamantla by bus to visit Chico. We soon found that our attire was not proper for us when we frightened Chico's family with our appearance! After a few days in town, and before Sandy and I left for the United States, Chico and I went to Tlaxcala, the state capital, accompanied by Chico's mother Juanita, his Uncle José and Sandy, to see the justice of peace. I was dressed in a light voilé dress (paid for by Juanita) with white shoes that we purchased on the way to Tlaxcala. With Sandy as our best man, Chico and I got married!

Chico and Sinikka, 1954.

Chapter 23

# Coming Home in 1955

**May 25, 1955**

Of the bus trip with Sandy between Mexico City and Nogales, Sonora, on the border with the United States, I remember little. It was about 1,600 miles and took us through several climate and vegetation zones. We descended from the mountain forests at 9,000 feet to sea level at Mazatlán, where I saw the Pacific Ocean for the first time. We saw the lush semi-tropical farmland of Sinaloa, which soon turned into desert.

**May 27, 1955**

Sandy and I walked across the border from Mexico to the United States with our luggage. For four days we stayed in Tucson, Arizona, with Dr. Earl Warner and his wife, who were Mona Dayton's (my camp leader in New Mexico) parents. On the day of our departure, Dr. Warner, a gentle, white-haired professor of physics, drove us outside the Tucson city limits, on the road to Los Angeles. We hitchhiked on a semitrailer that was carrying twenty-five tons of carrots. It was quite hot.

**June 1955**

The rides we got between Los Angeles and San Francisco were shorter and more varied, in "semis" and private cars. While Sandy's friends in Los Angeles had been a television writer and his wife, in Oakland we were received by a doctor and his wife, who scolded Sandy for not having let them know that he had a companion. I got the room meant for Sandy— for his punishment.

We traveled from San Francisco to Portland, Oregon, in the car of a friend of Sandy's, through the redwood forests and cooler country. In fact, it started snowing on the way, and we were cold in the car, which had a broken window. From Portland we drove to Forest Grove, where my Crownpoint camp leaders, Paul and Mona Dayton, lived with their family. A year earlier I had set foot on the North American continent in a place by the same name, Portland, but on the opposite side of the vast United States of America.

The Daytons lived in a three-story Castle School where Mona held kindergarten. There was a long slide from the second floor to the ground level—for anybody's use. The old house had a tower and many bay windows; I slept in a room on the second floor under an electric blanket for the very first time in my life. I worried a bit about electrocution.

## June 24, 1955

Four days later, after the good-byes, I found myself on a Greyhound bus again; first going north to Spokane, Washington, then east through the open lands of Montana and North Dakota—a few thousand kilometers before finding myself in Duluth, Minnesota. There I visited Kater's family, although Kater was still in Mexico. I watched television for the first time ever and wondered how people would get anything done because of television. Kater's family introduced me to a Finnish-American family with whom I stayed for a few days. They took me to the Finn Hall where, with a houseful of Finnish-Americans, we celebrated Juhannus with song and dance. I was asked to tell about Kater's and my experiences in Mexico and to sing the song about the "Cuckoo of Karelia," which moved them so much that they passed the hat and enriched my travel purse by forty dollars! I was also interviewed by a reporter, and my photo with my Otomi bag and Kater's sister appeared in a local paper.

## July 1955

After Minnesota my destination was Philadelphia, some 1,000 miles southeast, where I would report to the American Friends Service Committee and pick up my boat ticket to Europe. I spent a jolly day with my English friends Bunty and Joice, who were working there temporarily. From Philadelphia I went to New York. Bisse Öst, my Seitsikko friend, and her parents had just arrived as immigrants. It was fun to talk Finnish with Bisse; I even told her my secret—that I was married to Chico. I had not told anyone else about it, except Anja.

Boston seemed my second home, for Rose Perry was there. Lee Soherr, a volunteer from Zaragoza, had come from New York and lived close to Rose's apartment. I introduced them and helped Lee paint her apartment, listening to her romance. Rose was seeing John. (Both girls later married the men of their romances.) John took us to see a three-dimensional movie that made everybody scream. We swam and sailed on Charles River, but I was afraid of the waves crashing and the swinging boom.

My itinerary had been carefully timed for me to arrive at Quebec on the date of departure. In Boston I boarded the bus whose route followed the eastern coastline. When we arrived at the border, I got on a Canadian bus that took me to Quebec. Arriving at 2:00 AM, I didn't pick up my luggage until later. But when I went for it, I was told my luggage had not been dropped off but had gone on with the bus. There was not enough time to get it back. I had only a duffel bag containing a sleeping bag and a Mexican blanket that had been in use for twelve months without cleaning.

So, without my luggage, I sailed from Quebec to Cherbourg, France, on a Greek student boat holding six hundred passengers. It was very different from *Finntrader*, for the boat was old, meals were self-served, whatever there was. We even ran out of water. The cabins were small and crowded, but my companions were kind and gave me clothes to wear. The ship sailed down the St. Lawrence River and crossed the Gulf of St. Lawrence before entering the North Atlantic, which we crossed in ten days. During the trip I watched shipboard romances develop, but this time I stood on the sidelines, amused and wiser.

## August 1955

From Cherbourg in northern France at the English Channel, many of my shipmates—workcampers—took a train to Paris, where the Quakers had housing for us. We explored Paris on foot and by subway, saw the Seine with Notre Dame on its bank. We sat in the sidewalk cafés, enjoying wine and crunchy French bread. One evening I met a girl who, to my surprise, asked me about "Agustín." When I recovered I learned that she had been in Zaragoza during the summer camp and knew Chico. Our warehouse-type accommodations in Paris included a toilet without a bowl; metal footprints indicated where to stand. We joked about that a lot.

As many times before, my return trip to Finland went through Denmark, where the train was placed on tracks on the same ferry with the passengers, the cars zig-zagging to fit. This way one crossed two sounds, riding on the train between them across the island of Sjaelland. I kept an eye on my car, because I didn't want to lose my belongings. After crossing southern Sweden in a train, I took a luxury ferry from Stockholm to Helsinki, a trip of ten hours, paying only a deck fare and spending my night in a lounge chair.

It was wonderful to arrive at Helsinki's South Harbor basking in sunshine. To see my family and our comfortable wooden house, with large curtained windows through which I could see the green woods and fields, made me truly feel at home.

Chapter 24

# Leaving Finland

I had returned from a trip that had taken me not only to new countries, but to cultures vastly different from my own. After having experienced the Navajo Indian culture of New Mexico, the colorful rural life of Mexico, and the mountain culture of the Mexican Otomi Indians, I could now reflect upon them. I had stored information and impressions in the file labeled "to be handled later," and "later" was now. I could afford indulging in my experiences that had taken place in too rapid succession—for an entire year and more.

I rejoiced thinking about the many friends I had known. Anja, my sister, with whom I shared a room, would shake me awake, asking, "Whom are you now dreaming of. You're smiling!" I thought of Chico, with whom I had fallen in love and married, and relived precious moments with him. I wrote to him often, and he wrote to me.

One day soon after my return, as I sat in the garden swing, I viewed the abundance of growth in the plants Juhani, my brother, and I had started and felt somewhat accomplished. Cherishing the moment in the sun, I also knew that it would pass, that I had to find work, because I would be going back to Chico in Mexico within the year.

One of the benefits of having faced and managed new situations was a gain in self-reliance and aggressiveness. I applied for the position of translator in a company called EMS, which exported electrical products—a job for which I would not have dared apply before. I declared that I could handle English, German, and Spanish, in addition to my Finnish. I was tested in each, and I passed! The test in German was the most thrilling, for I had learned how the Germans started and ended their business letters from the correspondence I had had with the German shipping company that was handling my lost luggage in Canada!

My luggage arrived on a German ship, indeed, and one morning Mother and I boarded the freighter at the Jätkäsaari docks and claimed it. I enjoyed handing out the long-awaited gifts I had for my family, and I loved the smells that brought back memories. I had realized that in the temporary loss of my luggage, there had been a blessing in disguise, for without the correspondence with the German company, I wouldn't have passed the test at EMS.

Another translator in the company relieved me of writing anything in Swedish. It did not relieve me of the buzz from the boss and owner of the company, when he wanted me to take dictation. I got to be good in the use of dictionaries; once I even answered the letter of a Chilean copper mine in Spanish. And no one could check my writing!

For relief from job pressures, during my lunch hour, I often walked to KVT, the workcamp office, which I entered with my own key. I made myself tea and ate my sandwich in peace and quiet, sitting on the director's chair in a sunny spot. Many evenings I returned to work there and to participate in the programs of the organization.

Seitsikko, the Group of Seven met informally many times during the year I was in Finland. Nita had married and had a young son, whom we went to see on a very cold winter day. It was good to be with my friends with whom I had shared the war-time shortages, spent nights in the bomb shelters, written plays and danced to the music of my Dad's old Gramophone.

One of the records I had brought from Mexico was "Cerezo rosa" or "Pink Cherry Tree," a song about a beautiful spring, when "Una palabra te dí, una palabra me dió, amarnos siempre los dos y no dejarnos jamás . . . or "A word I gave you, you gave me yours to love one another forever and never leave each other. . . ." I lived on the thought of that song, and on Chico's letters. I worked hard and saved all I possibly could.

## January 1956

Many nights I came home at Mankkaa finding everyone in bed and food in the oven waiting for me. Mother would get up, and we talked. The snow was deep that winter, and many times a drift of snow had formed across the road, and I had to walk into it—up to my thighs. There were moments of despair at the bus stop when the wind pierced my covered face, cutting through my clothing. The full buses passed me without stopping.

## February 1956

I must mention that one day accidentally—or was it an accident—I ran into Ossi, Seitsikko's friend from the many excursions to Lake Urja. He stood at the corner near my work, as if waiting for me. We greeted each other calmly, without any hilarity. He had heard about my return, and I told him about my going back. Shivering and kicking our feet to keep them from freezing, our breaths steaming, we wished each other well, and departed quietly. The curtain fell on that part of my life.

## March 1956

As soon as the long general strike that caused great problems in transportation in Finland ended in March 1956, I wired my plans to Chico. Soon I took a Finnish freighter to North America. It was called *Finnpulp*, a handsome new ship taking hundreds of tons of paper and pulp across the ocean. In front were two icebreakers cracking ice and plowing through it, letting us slowly slide through to the open water of the Gulf of Finland. I left behind my solemn family that had accompanied me to my shipboard cabin with their flowers and reserved emotions. I had learned the art of reserving one's emotions, too, and only decades later realized how hard it must have been on my parents to see their first-born off to unknown parts of the world when the distances were enormous and travel expensive.

I reached Boston, snowless but cold, where Rose Perry, my friend from Camp Ruukinsalo in 1951, received me again. From Boston I traveled by bus through many southern states, where restrooms were set aside for "White" and "Colored," to the Mexican border. There at Reynosa, Chico, looking more worried than happy, and I fell into an embrace, happy but apprehensive about our future.

The eastern highway—the third of Mexico's roads in the north-south direction that I had traveled—was a scenic, winding road through rugged mountains and canyons. It passed by Ixmiquilpan, our camp town, before ending at Mexico City, reminding us of some wonderful times in the past. From Mexico City we traveled by train to Huamantla, Chico's hometown in the state of Tlaxcala, about 160 kilometers east. We arrived there in the middle of the night and carried my luggage through corn fields—on a short cut to Chico's home at Calle Victoria #26 Poniente.

As Chico opened the gate of his family's home, he welcomed me home with his reassuring hug. We had arrived—but was it I, the same I, who had recently left my family waving good-bye at the docks of the icy South Harbor in Finland?

*Chapter 25*

# Huamantla to FinnFest

More than three and a half decades have passed since March 1956 when, with the help of two icebreakers, my ship sailed for America and Chico, the man I had married ten months earlier, welcomed me home in Huamantla, Tlaxcala, Mexico.

The town soon discovered me as an English teacher they had been waiting for, and I taught those who came to me, and those who came to get me to teach their children in their large estate homes of high arches and massive gates. I also taught a few classes at the Federal Secondary School.

My contact with Finland was limited to letters from home and from friends, and to visits to the Consulate of Finland in Mexico City. When I needed to escape, that is where I went. As soon as I knew I was expecting a baby, I became a whirlwind of action, making baby clothes the Finnish way: from scratch and by hand, except for the sheets and a sleeping bag which Juanita, my mother-in-law, sewed in her bakery shop.

On December 6, 1956, when I was six months pregnant, I received an invitation to Finland's independence celebration to be held that evening in Mexico City. To fit into my best dress, I got Chico to tighten my maternity girdle. A friend of his gave me a lift to the bus terminal, and in three hours I arrived at the "Casa de los Amigos," which I knew so well, to make reservations for the night. Then a taxi took me to the Lomas de Chapultepec, an exclusive part of the giant city; all embassies were located there.

I was stunned at first and felt totally out of place for a moment, in my ponytail and ribbon, when I saw the glitter of the party: the crystal chandeliers, the diamonds and the champagne. The cream of society was there. Then, a feeling of defiance came over me, and I decided to enjoy myself. Who cared about the silk dresses and the furs when there was a splendid buffet table à la Finlandesa—loaded with wonderful eating, and Finnish music was playing! I found people from the consulate and had a good time talking Finnish with them. Of the buffet I remember only the tasty Finnish hot dogs, *nakit*, served with hot Finnish mustard.

That night I rested well in my bunk at the Casa and the next morning had breakfast with the others staying there, conversing in English. Then I made my rounds in the vibrant city, enjoying the trees and statues in Parque Juárez, and the bookstore in Bellas Artes. There, to my surprise, I found Aleksis Kivi's *The Seven Brothers* in Spanish and purchased the book for Chico for Christmas. I also bought yarn for my baby's sweater, coffee beans, and rye bread.

Our first son, Enrique or "Quique," was born on March 3, 1957, in Dr. Goya's private sanitarium in Huamantla. When he was five days old, Juanita, Chico's mother, and a friend of hers took us to a steam bath that was nearly as good as a Finnish sauna. In a bucket they carried fragrant, steaming herbs—for cleaning me after childbirth. I loved the treatment! The wrapping of my middle with straps of linen at home made me feel wonderful.

After two and a half years in Huamantla, on the 23rd of August, 1958, Chico, Quique (seventeen months old) and I flew to Nogales, Sonora, and the next day traveled to Tucson, Arizona, to the home of Paul Dayton and his family, my workcamp leaders from the New Mexico camp in 1954 who had moved from Oregon to Tucson. They were our sponsors and had secured a job for me as housemother in a fraternity house for Native Americans and a job for Chico at a first-class inn. There he learned the rudiments of fine French cuisine from a temperamental French lady.

Just before Christmas I was invited to appear with a church choir on television, singing "O, come all ye faithful" ("Nyt riemuiten tänne kiiru-husti tulkaa . . .") in Finnish.

On the 14th of April, 1959, my friend and classmate Pirkko Viljanen came for a visit, finding me nine months pregnant. At midnight I woke her up, along with Chico and our neighbor Freddie, for my labor pains had started. Freddie, a sophisticated, unmarried lady, sixty years of age, got so excited about it all that she ran a red light driving me to the hospital. An hour later when Dina was born, the doctor said to me, "Sinikka, you're going to have another baby!" And Lisa was born. Twins!

A group of "Friends" or Quakers whom we had gotten to know, took us under their wings, providing us with goods and services and plenty of arms for carrying the babies. There were, however, moments of silent despair when the two tiny babies were crying, and Quique, barely two, demanded much of my attention, and I was tired. How I longed for the closer family and extra arms available at all hours in Mexico. (In Finland Mother had been "helping" us by wringing her hands in desperation!)

Our "Halcyon Years" were the twelve years spent in our home on Halcyon Road, an old house with a mature garden with tall and shady trees. There were plenty of hiding places for the children under the water tank covered with yellow jasmine, in the oleander bushes and in the garage with two secret compartments.

With the help and encouragement of Freddie and Chico I enrolled at the University of Arizona in the fall of 1960, as a foreign student. Chela, a friend from Huamantla, came to take care of the children. When I had to learn to accompany forty children's songs on the piano, all three of our children learned them; I tried everything I was learning on them. In my music class at the university, I demonstrated that a song in minor key didn't have to sound sad, by teaching the Finnish folksong "My sweetheart is beautiful inspite of . . ." ("Minun kultani kaunis on vaikk'on . . .") accompanied by a large bulletin board that had a log cabin and lumbermen cutting down trees.

By the time our son Tom was born in October 1963, we had Finnish friends in town: Drs. Maija and Alvar Wilska and their two children, plus Ulla-Maija Aaltonen, whom I met in a psychology class. In May 1964, I received my Bachelor of Arts degree in Elementary Education, and became a citizen of the United States of America. A week after my graduation, my mother came for her first visit, connecting us to Finland anew. During her stay, Tommy was baptized, and I found a job teaching Spanish part-time. And we got the idea of going to Finland.

Nine years after leaving Finland, nine years of busy living, the children and I flew on an Icelandic Airlines propeller aircraft via Reykjavik to Helsinki. When I saw below me the tranquil, dark clusters of woods, green patches of fields, and countless lakes glimmering in the sunshine, my heart was aflutter and my eyes became cloudy. It was wonderful to be back! Everyone was there to meet us: my parents, sisters, brothers, relatives. The first one to receive me was my father; with open arms he approached me, flowers in his hand and tears in his eyes.

The minute we got to Mankkaa, Quique (eight), Dina and Lisa (six) and Tommy (eighteen months) ran upstairs to meet my sister Anja's children: Ari, Arja and Lissu, whose ages were about the same as our children's. There was no difficulty with the language, but to my astonishment, the children spoke in Finnish and English and used command forms from the beginning. (In textbooks imperatives are found at the end of the book.) "Come here!" "Tule tänne!" "Like this." "Näin." "Let's go!" "Mennään!"

Although there were only ten sunny days during our two-months' stay, we enjoyed being there. Ari and Quique took swimming lessons in the ice-cold ocean, after first warming up thoroughly in the sauna. We went to the beach to build sandcastles and to sun ourselves at every chance we had between the clouds. When the clouds covered the sun, we looked for our towels for warmth. And never swam!

In the yard the kids discovered bluish clay with which they could make bowls. There were bicycles to ride, soccer to play with Ukki (my dad), a pond to visit and fields to run on. And there were very many visits—endless cups of coffee to drink and pulla-bread to eat! Street cars and elevators were a novelty, and Mother's tiny potatoes a favorite, as were her satin comforters.

One day in Helsinki, a Gypsy lady stopped us and worriedly questioned me as to where we were going. She looked over the kids and demanded to know who their father was! With their father's tan skin and brown hair, our children must have resembled Gypsy children!

Seitsikko, the group of seven, met one pretty summer evening at Magi's summer place. It was as if we never had been away from each other.

Tuula, my little sister, at sixteen, played with the kids a lot, carrying them on her back, one after another. It was Pentti's, my "little" brother's turn to be in the Army. We saw him in his long, gray mantle when he had time off and came home—struggling to take a step forward from his seven adoring nieces and nephews, who captured him at the gate.

One weekend my brother Juhani (married to Ella and father of Henry and Anne) drove eleven of us stuffed in his tiny English-made Mini Minor car to a cabin at the seashore. There we lived in the lap of nature, picking blueberries, fishing, rowing, taking saunas daily—for a week. Tuula, Anja and I would sit by the window looking toward the bay, enjoying the quiet after the children had gone to bed. The peace of a summer evening settled over the water, and fog formed clouds on it. On the opposite side of the bay we could see lights twinkling in the windows of other cabins. I was so happy I was there.

The farewells were inevitable, and the delay so long at the airport that our children were sprawled on the benches, asleep. When it finally came time to board the plane, I could not find our tickets! We got on only because Tauri Aaltio himself, the director of Suomi Society, was there and remembered us from the time we arrived in Finland.

At Kennedy Airport we were received by Chico with open arms, and we rejoiced being together again. After three and a half days on the road, we reached our home in Tucson, Arizona, where the giant saguaros grow and where the sun always shines.

In May 1968, my sister Tuula, nineteen, arrived to spend a year with us. We showed her the wonders of the Sunset Crater and the Petrified Forest in northern Arizona. The Grand Canyon was next, but it did not show itself, but was covered with massive clouds and surrounded by snow.

Tuula's visit brought a great piece of luck to us, when a clerk at the post office one day spoke to her in Finnish, inviting all of us to the Finnish-American Club's Midsummer party (Juhannus). That was twenty-four years ago. The club and its members became an axis around which my family has ever since rotated. There have hardly been any Christmases without at least one of us performing something in Finnish. There hasn't been a year I did not hold an office; I was president of the club for seven interesting years.

The Juhannus parties held on our patio have provided food and drink, music, sauna and swimming—and of course, pleasant company. Finland's flag is always hoisted for the occasion: the blue of the summer sky and white of winter's snow.

Tuula's presence had reinforced Finnishness into my family; we used Finnish names for foods, and exclaimed, "Herranjestas!" instead of "My gosh!" Christmas would not be Christmas without the arrival of a package that smelled of ryebread and woollens. And the red three-candle candlestick has always decorated both the Finnish Club's Little Christmas (Pikku joulu) and our Christmas table. There's always raisin pulla, ginger snaps, and cinnamon rolls made the Finnish way (korvapuusti) and holiday banquets have a dish of traditional rutabaga casserole. Many of our cats had names like Kissa, Musti, Pikku, Renttu.

We have not been without Mexican influence in our daily lives either, and the American way was always with us. Yet Finnish customs have underlaid our lives. The numerous long-term visitors from both countries have had their effect, making us a tri-cultural family. Once my mother and Angelita, Chico's niece, were with us at the same time, neither one understanding the other one's language, yet they got along fine when the rest of us were away. Mother taught Angelita to embroider pillowcases, and together the two helped one of our cats in birthing—the first time for all three participants.

Almost every year we have a visitor from Finland, and every other year one of us goes there. Quique flew there in 1971, Tommy and I in 1973, Chico and I in 1975. My niece Lissu and Aunt Jöppe arrived with Mother in 1977, and Anja came to swim and to listen to the cicadas in 1979. I have lost the count of my trips to Finland, but in 1981 Lisa, my daughter, and I went together; Lisa to attend the Suomi Society's Cultural Seminar for three weeks, and I to have fun with my friends and with my expanding Finnish family. We returned home with a Finnish string instrument, a twenty-six-string kantele.

In February of 1975, after a pause of twenty years in writing my diary, I started anew. In the spring I received from Anne Nolan Clark, a local author, a copy of her manuscript about a Finnish family; we met before she went to Finland to do research, and she met my family while there. What made it especially interesting for me was that the main character in her book had the name of my younger brother Pentti.

In June 1975, Quique (fifteen) built a sauna with an electrical heater. It became a refuge on Friday nights for Chico and me; the steam helped us relax from the weekly toil and it made us feel renewed. The kids enjoyed having a sauna and a swim whenever their busy schedule allowed.

At my new school on the foothills of the Santa Catalina Mountains the "Dungeons and Dragons" craze was taking place in 1981. The game is based on mythological characters, some of them from the Finnish national epic Kalevala. In the game the players struggle through dangers, defeating the enemy with mythological weapons, or lose and are sent to the dungeon. The magic of the Finnish mythical heroes, such as Väinämöinen, the old wise man, and Ilmarinen, the smith that wrought the magic mill Sampo, was in their singing. Väinämöinen could sing his opponent into the ground, or change him into an animal.

In 1981 the tradition of the "European Fair" got started in my classroom. Later the idea spread to other sixth grade rooms at our school, and eventually it was officially added to the curriculum of all sixth grades in our school district. Small groups of students selected a European country and did research on it. They prepared maps, charts, and pictures to enhance their project. For the fair, they prepared a booth made of desks or large cardboard boxes. Portuguese sausage, Czechoslovakian dumpling soup, English tea and scones, paella from Spain, spaghetti from Italy, and Finnish Big-Eye cheese (*Tahko juusto*) and herring (*silli*) on Rye Crisp were offered. The Monaco booth had a roulette, and the Spanish booth supplied Flamenco dancing, and Finnish music was played all through the day in the background.

During my 1984 winter trip to Finland I visited an elementary school in Tapiola, the garden city by Helsinki, introducing the English classes to the idea of having pen pals in Arizona. When I found the school surrounded by high walls of snow and some students playing ice hockey on the school rink, I wished my students in Tucson had been there! The pen pal idea took and much fun followed in writing and receiving letters and pictures. "Ghostbusters" formed a link between the youngsters of the two countries—and so did the rock group "Motley Crue." (Mötley Crüe)

One year my classmate, friend, and colleague, Thelma, from Helsinki, came to Tucson to learn about approaches to the teaching of writing in schools. Dina, Lisa (both now teachers), and I made arrangements for her to visit elementary, junior high and high schools. Thelma saw plenty and returned to Finland with a suitcase full of materials on the subject.

Since 1975, our club has participated in "Tucson Meet Yourself," an annual multicultural festival. Over a weekend in October, we set up our booth with a log cabin look, among the many other booths, and sell pulla, sima, cinnamon rolls, Karelian piirakkas, meatballs, cabbage casserole, and blueberry and apple squares. Our singing group performs Finnish folksongs on the stage in the non-stop program, and some of us in our national costumes join the parade to represent Finland with its flag. Our sales of food at Tucson Meet Yourself provide us with funds for scholarships (Salolampi Language Village) and donations (Suomi College Archives).

In 1983, in cooperation with the Southwest Folklore Center of the University of Arizona, our Finnish Club showed Professor Loukinen's documentary "Finnish-American Lives." There we met Arizona's honorary consul Frank Smith, who, with his Finnish wife, Kirsti, from then on started attending our meetings and parties. Many of us have been to the

Smiths' home in Phoenix for receptions in honor of either a parting consul general or a visiting ambassador. Once we met Armi Kuusela, the Finnish Miss Universe of 1952.

FinnFest USA was the brain child of Tauri Aaltio, then the director of Suomi Society (the one who let my children and me on the plane at Helsinki Airport in 1965 without tickets I couldn't find). He had traveled widely among the Finns abroad on many continents and knew of their nostalgic loyalty to their mother country, whose customs and culture they still appreciated and celebrated with enthusiasm. Sensing a need to bring everyone together so that they could identify, share, and rejoice with one another, the idea of the FinnFest was born. FinnFest has widened our horizons and deepened our appreciation for our inheritance and helped us identify ourselves as Finnish among the millions of Americans of many ethnic and cultural backgrounds.

The first FinnFest was held in August 1983 in Minneapolis, Minnesota. Since my long-time friend Kater Nelson lived in nearby Roseville, I had lodging and transportation provided for me. I spent three days among strangers attending lectures, workshops, browsing through book sales and the market place—loving it. At the banquet of 800 Finnish-Americans I got to know people, and, dressed in my Karelian costume, I proudly represented the Finns of Arizona.

From a lecturer I learned that the "melting pot" concept had never come to be, but that the different ethnic groups had left a permanent mark in the tapestry that is America today. From many speakers I learned about the struggle of the early Finnish immigrants, especially with the English language.

Later I was nominated by Tauri Aaltio to the Board of Directors, and I became a member and part of a very exciting group of representatives, who have become annually renewed personal friends.

At Suomi College in Hancock, Michigan, we celebrated the 150th anniversary of the publishing of the Kalevala, the Finnish epic poem. At Berkeley in 1986 we met to celebrate "Finns of the West." The fabulous Opening Ceremonies included first-class folkdancing by both Finnish-American and Finnish folkdance groups.

The following year we returned to Michigan—to Detroit—to celebrate Michigan's 150th birthday and Finland's 70th year of independence. A superb play about the "Copper Country" was seen.

In 1988 Wilmington, Delaware, received us next to celebrate the 350th anniversary of the first Finnish settlement in America. Among the exciting things for me at this FinnFest was meeting Finnish dignitaries, such as Matti Ahde, the Speaker of the Finnish Parliament, who awarded to us the medal of Suomi Society, honoring our work among the Finnish-Americans. I also met Martti Häikiö, the new director of Suomi Society, and Matti Nykänen, the three-gold medal champion of ski jumping in

Sinikka showing off the Soumi Society metal (for the work among Finnish-Americans) at FinnFest '88 in Delaware.

the Winter Olympics of that year. The topping on the cake was meeting my childhood friend Bisse, one of the "Seitsikko" girls—after thirty-three years.

By the time we went to Seattle for the FinnFest of 1989, FinnFest had become an absolute must for me. I went to meet my "annual" friends. In Seattle I enjoyed nature more than anywhere else: the boats on the sound, the locks, the jumping salmon, and the pink fireweeds that reminded me of my childhood years. At the University of Washington the highlight performance for me was the slide show with narration called "A Memory of Finland" by Marja Eloheimo. She received a silent standing ovation, indicating our elation with misty eyes, and exclamations of "How wonderful! Thank you, thank you!"

Merja Laukontaus-Soria delighted us at Suomi College in 1990 with her wonderful folksinging and kantele and accordion playing. (She planned to perform for us in Tucson on our 25th anniversary dinner. Unfortunately, because of an illness, she had to cancel her trip.) At Suomi College, best of all I enjoyed the musical drama about Lemminkäinen, a Kalevala hero, written and produced by Melvin Kangas.

One of the highlights at the FinnFest at Lake Worth, Florida in 1991, was the Writers' Workshop conducted by Professor Richard Impola, an inspiring speaker on Finnish-American matters, and a writer and translator of Finnish literature. (His latest translation: *The Seven Brothers* by Aleksis Kivi.*) At that conference I came to know Mavis Hiltunen-Biesanz, whose book *A Finnish-American Girlhood* I had read and much appreciated. We talked and together enjoyed a church concert given by the Finnair Choir.

This year of 1992, as FinnFest returns to Minnesota to celebrate its 100th birthday, as well as Finland's 75th, the programs and festivities will take place in Duluth. In the past we celebrated "Origins, Traditions, Reunion" in the amazingly "Finnish" community of Fitchburg, Massachusetts, where the Helsinki Polytech Choir moved us to tears, and where I danced dizzying polkas and jenkas after decades without.

All the wonderful ingredients of life for me have always circled around the Finnishness in me. I have tried to be a tradition bearer for my children and grandchildren, yet realizing their other inheritances. I hope the hundreds of students I one time taught remember me as a guide of a tour of nations that have produced the fibers in the quilt that has made America what it is.

In Tucson, Arizona, in place of majestic pine forests and birch trees we have fields of sweet-smelling, sun-heated burrsage, and giant saguaro cacti that with their beauty inspire awe and symbolize endurance beyond man's longevity.

---

*The book has been translated into English before—many times. Richard's is especially written for Finnish-Americans.

# Glossary

*agua miel*, sweet juice from the maguey (agave)
*cántaro*, earthen jug for water
*Casa de los Amigos*, The AFSC (Quakers) House in Mexico City
*comal*, hot plate made of thin clay
*Hertta* and *Heluna*, common names for cows
*Kalevala*, the Finnish national epic poem
*KVT*, *Kansainvälinen Vapaaehtoinen Työleirijärjestö*—International
    Voluntary Workcamp Organization
*kessu*, Finnish home-grown tobacco
*Laskiainen*, Shrovetide, mainly used for sledding
*Lemminkäinen*, The lover-boy of the Kalevala
*lotta*, an Army nurse in gray uniform
*Little Christmas*, Pikku joulu, the first advent, used for company parties in
    anticipation of Christmas
*maestro*, teacher, conductor, anyone directing others
*mansikka*, strawberry
*Markka*, a Finnish coin, worth an American quarter ('92)
*milpa*, corn field (Mexico)
*Mennään!* Let's go!
*mustikka*, blueberry
*nakit*, tasty, slender Finnish hot dogs
*näin*, like this
*pesäpallo*, Finnish baseball
*piirakka*, pie (Karelian pies are filled with rice)
*pippuri*, pepper
*pulla*, yeast bread containing cardamom
*pässi*, ram
*pulque*, fermented beer-like drink from the agave

*rebozo*, a shawl (Mexico)
*Seitsikko*, the group of seven: Anja, Bisse, Magi, Laila, Inge, Sinikka and
    Nita
*silver tea*, hot water mixed with milk
*taco*, anything wrapped in a tortilla, usually beans
*tamales*, meat, spices and corn dough wrapped in corn husks or banana
    leaves, then cooked
*Tule tänne!* Come here!
*tupa*, the main room of any farm house
*Vappu*, the First of May, the Finnish Labor Day, celebrated mostly for the
    coming of summer
*Väinämöinen*, the wise old man, the main character in the Kalevala; with
    magical singing power

The author. Anyone who has lived in Arizona for thirty years is considered
"native." Yet Sinikka Garcia, aided by many Finnish connections, such as
FinnFest USA, has kept Finnishness alive within her family and the
Finnish-Americans of Tucson, Arizona.